What former Roman Catholic priests and nuns are saying about *Talking with Catholic Friends and Family*

Talking with Catholic Friends and Family is a refreshingly accurate and readable presentation of Catholic thinking in laymen's terms. McCarthy has chosen typical, not exceptional, examples of his conversations with real people and interwoven biblical with Catholic doctrine to create a brightly contrasting mosaic. I recognized every one of the situations and couldn't help thinking as I read: *What oft was thought, but ne'er so well expressed.*

Mary Kraus
Former Franciscan Sister

Talking with Catholic Friends and Family goes to the heart of the matter. The author has a unique gift for explaining complex issues in an uncomplicated way. I wholeheartedly recommend this book both to seeking Catholics and to those who would help them.

Vince O'Shaughnessy
Former Diocesan Priest

If you like true stories, you'll love *Talking with Catholic Friends and Family*. It's about real people and events (including some related to my own life). I highly recommend this book to anyone interested in the spiritual needs of Catholics.

Bob Bush
Former Jesuit Priest

Talking with Catholic Friends and Family will make you laugh and will make you cry. A collection of real-life stories, it illustrates both the humorous and the tragic sides of living life as a Catholic. May God use this book to bring many into the full light of the gospel.

Bartholomew F. Brewer
Former Discalced Carmelite Priest

Talking with Catholic Friends and Family is a down-to-earth account of the beliefs, hopes, doubts, and fears of the Catholic people. Loaded with practical insights from God's Word, it provides the truth that sets people free.

Wilma Sullivan
Former Sister of Mercy

Through the mouths of Catholics, this book presents what is really going on inside Roman Catholicism. A valuable tool for those who want to understand Catholicism.

Joseph Tremblay
Former Priest of the Oblates of Mary Immaculate

This book is an excellent resource. Loaded with carefully researched information, it provides a biblical analysis of where Roman Catholicism has gone wrong. Through it you will better understand how Catholics think and be able to explain to them the good news of Jesus Christ.

Yvonne Freeman
Former Sister of the Holy Family

I read this book with enthusiasm and identification. Enthusiasm because the author has explained so well how the doctrines of Roman Catholicism affect the lives of the Catholic people. Identification because the many stories found in it caused me to recall my own search for God as a Catholic nun.

Rocio Pestaña Segovia
Former Franciscan Nun

In sharing the gospel with Catholics, I have long prayed for a book that would clearly explain the good news of Jesus Christ through stories. I thank God that such a book now exists. In *Talking with Catholic Friends and Family* the reader will find the message of God's grace spoken in love. To God be the glory.

Richard Bennett
Former Dominican Priest

Talking *with* Catholic Friends *and* Family

JAMES G. McCARTHY

HARVEST HOUSE PUBLISHERS

EUGENE, OREGON

Links to each of the Internet websites mentioned in this book are maintained by the author at the ministry website of Good News for Catholics, www.gnfc.org.

TALKING WITH CATHOLIC FRIENDS AND FAMILY
Copyright © 1999/2005 by James G. McCarthy
Published by Harvest House Publishers
Eugene, Oregon 97402
www.harvesthousepublishers.com

Library of Congress Cataloging-in-Publication Data
McCarthy, James G., 1952-
    Talking with Catholic friends and family / James G. McCarthy.
        p. cm.
    Includes bibliographical references (p.   ) and index.
    ISBN-13: 978-0-7369-1669-1
    ISBN-10: 0-7369-1669-5 (pbk.)
    1. Evangelicalism—Relations—Catholic Church. 2. Catholic Church—Relations—Evangelicalism. 3. Witness bearing (Christianity)
    I. Title.
    BR1641.C37M33 2005
    248'.5'088282—dc22   2005004200

Printed in the United States of America

05 06 07 08 09 10 11 12 / VP-MS / 10 9 8 7 6 5 4 3 2 1

Contents

A Vast Mission Field

Over one billion people strong, and more all the time, they make up one-sixth of the world's population. They are Central and South Americans (89 percent), Europeans (41 percent), Oceanians (27 percent), North Americans (24 percent), Africans (17 percent), and Asians (3 percent). They live in Brazil (135 million), Mexico (84 million), the United States (70 million), and many other countries. They are Hispanic, Filipino, French, Irish, Polish, Italian, German, Vietnamese, Indian, Korean, Chinese—you name it; they're it. They're your neighbor, your grocer, your doctor, your local politician, the attendant who takes your money at the gas station. They're the professional athlete on television, the big-time criminal in the papers, the actor/director with a shelf full of Academy Awards. They may be your mother, your father, sister, brother, aunt and uncle, the whole clan. From the pope in his jet to the penniless immigrant newly arrived in your country, they're the people all around you. Collectively they form the membership of the largest organization on earth. They're Catholics, meaning *universal*, and as their name indicates, they're everywhere.

They are also a people who need your help. A long time ago—it'd be hard to say when—the bishops of the Catholic Church veered off course, taking the Catholic people with them. At first the errors were small, but with time they accumulated. Eventually priests, theologians, and even average churchgoing Catholics noticed they were in uncharted waters. Some complained, calling for reform. They received only trouble for their efforts. Headstrong and angry, the bishops of the Catholic Church arrested some, executed others. They called a council, and formally denounced the dissenters as heretics, putting them outside the Church and the salvation it offered. The bishops codified their many errors, making them dogmas (irrevocable doctrines that all Catholics must believe). The result is that today, some 450 years later, the gospel of Jesus Christ is no longer preached from Catholic pulpits, and the people, though often zealous for the practice of religion, are for the most part unsaved and without a true knowledge of God.

This book is about how you can help them. It is written for Christians who love God and love the Catholic people. It's a book about how to understand Catholics and how to communicate to them the gospel of Jesus Christ.

Part One

Talking to Catholics About Salvation

1

Nobody Knows

any Catholics believe their church is the biggest and the best. The original! Each week at Mass they profess to be members of the "one, holy, catholic, and apostolic church." Christ instituted it. Their bishops are the successors of the 12 apostles; their pope the successor of Saint Peter himself, to whom Christ said, "Thou art Peter; and upon this rock I will build my church" (Matthew 16:18, Douay Rheims Version). Within the Catholic religion alone is found the *fullness* of revealed truth and salvation. At the same time, most Catholics readily admit they're not sure what will happen to them when they die.

"Nobody knows if they're going to heaven," said a Catholic woman in her thirties visiting our church. Her name was Jane DeLisi. Along with her husband, John, and another Catholic couple, Roger and Beverly, she was looking for answers. "No one knows what the next life holds," Jane said. "How could they?"

"You can know," said O. Jean Gibson, a friend who was with me.

"You can't," Jane insisted. "Nobody knows, not even the pope."

Jean turned in his Bible to 1 John 5:13, and asked Jane to read it.

"These things I have written to you who believe in the name of the Son of God," she read, "in order that you may have eternal life." When she finished, she looked up as if to say, "So?"

11

Jean looked equally puzzled. Taking the Bible from her, he glanced at it, then returned it to her. "Read it again," he said.

"These things I have written to you," Jane read, "who believe in the name of the Son of God, in order that you may have eternal life." This time she continued staring at the verse, trying to figure out what he thought was so significant.

"Try it again," he said.

Again Jane read 1 John 5:13, this time slower. "These things I have written to you who believe in the name of the Son of God"—she paused long enough to see if Jean was going to object, then continued—"in order that you may have eternal life."

"You're leaving out part of the verse," he said.

"I am?" Jane was baffled. A teacher with eight years' experience in the Catholic parochial school system, she *taught* reading! Now she was being told that despite three attempts, she couldn't get a simple sentence straight. Not easily deterred, Jane gave it another try. "These things I have written to you who believe in the name of the Son of God, in order that you may have eternal life." Realizing she had read the verse the same way again, she decided not to wait to be corrected. "I don't see it. What am I doing wrong?"

"You're leaving out the word *know*," Jean said. "Isn't the word *know* in the verse?"

Jane took another look. "I guess it is. I can't see how I could have missed it, but there it is."

"Okay, read it again," he said. "This time the whole verse."

"'These things I have written to you who believe in the name of the Son of God, in order *that you may know* that you have eternal life.' That *is* different," she said with a smile. "I didn't think anyone could *know* they were going to heaven."

Jean wasn't about to stop there. "Who may know they have eternal life?" he asked.

"You who believe in the name of the Son of God," she answered, reading the verse.

"That's right. So the question becomes, Do you believe in the Son of God?"

"I think so," she said. "I'm not sure."

For the next 90 minutes, Jean explained the biblical way of salvation to Jane, John, Roger, and Beverly. When he finished, all four placed their trust in Christ to save them.

Why Jane Can't Read

Undoubtedly, Jane was nervous the evening she misread 1 John 5:13 four times. It is also true that the wording of the verse is somewhat awkward. But the main reason she had so much difficulty reading it had to do with *what* the verse says. The idea that anyone could know that he or she was going to heaven was so foreign to her thinking that Jane simply skipped that part of the verse. She read it the way she expected it to read, making it say what she believed to be true.

Like Jane, most Catholics are unsure what will happen in the next life. This was vividly demonstrated when we were filming *Catholicism: Crisis of Faith*, a documentary examining the teachings of Roman Catholicism. We set up our camera outside Saint Patrick's Cathedral in New York City. There we interviewed Catholics leaving Mass. We asked them how they hoped to get to heaven and whether they thought they were going to make it.

"I sure hope so," Jack, a Catholic from North Dakota, answered.

Catherine, Jack's wife, agreed. "I hope so, too. But there will be someone else judging that."

"Everybody hopes," a woman from France told us. "Every Catholic hopes."

"You don't know what's going to happen until you get there," Norman, a resident of New York City, explained. "You might find a surprise waiting for you."

Joe from Baltimore was also visiting the cathedral that day. When we asked him if he expected to go to heaven, he answered, "I hope to.

Yes, I expect to. And I hope to. My wife is, I hope, up there. She died two years ago." When we asked him whether he *knew* he was going to heaven, he made an important distinction. "No," he answered. "I don't know. But I hope to. I don't think you can know the future. We hope we wind up in heaven. That's what we strive for."

Hoping, but not *knowing*, is the consensus among Catholics. A few years back, Cardinal John O'Connor of New York put it this way:

> Church teaching is that I don't know, at any given moment, what my eternal future will be. I can hope, pray, do my very best—but I still don't know. Pope John Paul II doesn't know absolutely that he will go to heaven, nor does Mother Teresa of Calcutta.[1]

One Catholic woman compared salvation to a bank account. You open the account when you're baptized, she said. Receiving the sacraments and performing good works is like adding money to that account. Committing a venial sin takes money out. A mortal sin bankrupts your account. In order to restore it to a positive balance, you must receive the sacrament of confession. Whether you go to heaven or hell is determined by the status of your account at the moment of death. If you have money in the bank, so to speak, you go to heaven. If not, you go to hell. And since nobody knows what his final balance will be at the moment of death, no one can know where he is going until he gets there.

Why Catholics Don't Know

Catholics don't know where they're going because from the day they are baptized until the day they die, they are on probation with God. Life is a trial during which a person must prove through his faith and obedience that he is worthy of heaven. Eternal life hangs in the balance. The Catholics we interviewed outside Saint Patrick's

Cathedral confirmed this when we asked them *how* they hoped to get to heaven.

"I hope to get to heaven," Julia, a Catholic woman coming out of the cathedral, told us, "by leading a good life and being honest with people."

Norman gave us a list of requirements to get to heaven: "Prayer, perseverance, doing what the Catholic Church teaches. You have to be honest, do good, go to confession, go to church, and treat your neighbors as good as you can."

Sharon from New York state also spoke of salvation as dependent upon the accomplishment of a list of activities: "Do good works. Believe in Jesus Christ. Try to practice your beliefs and your religion in your everyday life. Do things for humanity."

Joyce from Michigan summarized the requirements as "Follow your Ten Commandments. Live a good Christian life. Love everyone."

Did these Catholics think they could accomplish these things well enough to get into heaven? Most were quick to say they weren't so sure.

"Well, I got a lot of work to do," said Ray, a Catholic from Ohio. "I hope to go to heaven when I die. I hope and pray to God that I do. And if I don't, I know it will be because of something I did that I shouldn't have done."

Fran, a Catholic woman from Seneca Falls, New York, put it this way: "I hope the good things I do on earth will sit well with God, and He'll look favorably on it, and take me into heaven."

"If you did right you'll get there," another man explained. "If you haven't done right by your Man, you'll get your just rewards, maybe in hell, maybe in purgatory."

Knowing Where You're Going

When we asked Pat, a Catholic woman from Ohio whom we interviewed outside of Saint Patrick's Cathedral, how she hoped to get to heaven, she answered, "Catholicism isn't any different than any other religion. If you obey the Ten Commandments, I think you've got a pretty good chance. You can't go wrong with the Ten Command-ments."

At least with regard to her first comment, Pat is correct. Catholicism isn't any different from most religions. Whether it's Islam, Hinduism, a mixture of Chinese religions, or one of the Christian sects such as Mor-monism or the Jehovah's Witnesses, most religions are basically the same. Like Roman Catholicism, they all teach that if you live a good life on earth, you have a pretty good chance of enjoying blessings in heaven.

Biblical Christianity stands apart. It teaches that "no one is good except God alone" (Mark 10:18), that "all our righteous deeds are like a filthy garment" (Isaiah 64:6). True Christianity teaches that sinners can be accepted by God only through the righteous work of Christ (Romans 3:21-26; 2 Corinthians 5:21). It proclaims a Savior who paid our penalty for us with His own life (Mark 10:45; 1 Peter 2:24). It tells of God's offer of eternal life to anyone who repents and believes (Mark 1:15; John 3:16; Ephesians 2:8-9). Those who accept this free gift can *know* that they are going to heaven because their acceptance before God is in Christ, not in themselves.

The Lord Jesus assured His disciples of their salvation, saying, "Rejoice that your names are recorded in heaven" (Luke 10:20). He said of those who believe in Him, "I give eternal life to them, and they will never perish; and no one will snatch them out of My hand. My Father, who has given them to Me, is greater than all; and no one is able to snatch them out of the Father's hand" (John 10:28-29). The Holy Spirit also participates in guaranteeing the future of the redeemed. At the moment of salvation, the Spirit comes to dwell in each believer "as a pledge of our inheritance, with a view to the redemption of God's own possession, to the praise of His glory" (Ephesians 1:14).

Some call the confidence that you are saved *rash presumption*, and they would be right if salvation were dependent, even in part, upon our righteous deeds. Believing the promises of Scripture, however, is not rash presumption, but faith in God's Word. It's doing what Jane DeLisi found so difficult the night we spoke with her. It's allowing the Scriptures to speak for themselves, taking God at His word, and believing what He says.

Recently, I spoke with Jane. I asked her if she has doubts about whether she will go to heaven.

"No," Jane answered without hesitation, "not since that night. I know that I believe in Jesus. I know that He died for me. I know that if I died tonight, I would be in heaven. And that gives me great peace."

2

Are You Calling Me a Pharisee?

I knew something was wrong the moment Mrs. Murphy's teenage daughter opened the door. The Murphys, a large Irish Catholic family I had been visiting regularly for several weeks, were interested in learning about the Bible, so I was surprised when the young girl greeted me with a tense hello and a warning: "You really got my mom mad the last time you were here!"

From the tone of her voice, it was clear that the daughter had also taken offense at something I had said, but my mind was blank as to what it could be. As she led me into the living room, I quickly tried to recall my visit two weeks earlier. But the effort was unnecessary. There in the center of the room stood Mrs. Murphy. She was waiting for me.

"Are you calling me a Pharisee?" she demanded.

Normally an exceptionally pleasant person, the bite in her voice told me that she was out for blood. "What do you mean?" I asked sheepishly. "I never called you a Pharisee."

She took a quick breath and just as she was about to launch her offensive, she changed her mind and stormed out of the room in a huff.

"I'm sorry, but I don't know what this is about," I called after her.

My plea went unheard. Mrs. Murphy was gone. "What's this all about?" I asked her daughter.

"She said you called her a Pharisee."

"I wouldn't do that," I said, pleading innocence.

"She said it was something you wrote down and gave her last time you were here."

"So that's it!" I said, finally realizing what had happened. During my previous visit, Mrs. Murphy and I had talked about the meaning of sin. I had tried to help her understand that she was a sinner who needed to be saved, but she would have nothing of it.

"I've lived a good, decent life," Mrs. Murphy had objected.

"All our righteous deeds are like a filthy garment," I had told her.

"What've I ever done?" she asked.

"Have you always put God first?"

"Of course!"

"Have you ever used God's name in vain?"

"No."

"Have you ever lied?"

"What would I have to lie about?"

"Have you ever stolen anything?"

"No!" she answered confidently.

"Have you ever had an unclean thought?" I asked, fully aware that I was treading on sacred ground. In Irish families, mothers with six or more children like Mrs. Murphy are considered living saints. Predictably, she lost her patience.

"I don't know what's wrong with you. Your generation might be obsessed with sex, but I don't have those kinds of thoughts."

Realizing the topic had progressed as far as it was going to that day, I decided to make a tactical retreat. On a notepad, I wrote out a Scripture reference for Mrs. Murphy and handed it to her. "Take a look at this passage sometime," I suggested.

Mrs. Murphy, believing that she had successfully defended her state of sinlessness against my assault, accepted the note cheerfully. Her warm farewell as I departed left me unprepared for the hostile reception I was now receiving, two weeks later.

"It wasn't me who called your mother a Pharisee," I told her daughter. "It was God through the Scriptures."

Deceived as to Their Sins

Mrs. Murphy is typical of a great number of Catholics. A hardworking mother living a simple life, she viewed herself a good person. Her conscience may have troubled her from time to time, making her feel guilty about something she had said or done. But any idea that she was a sinner who had offended God and deserved eternal punishment never crossed her mind. Her Church, her culture, and her own heart had convinced her of that. She may not be perfect—who is?—but she certainly wasn't a bad person. She was no sinner, and woe betide the person who dared say otherwise!

For some people it wouldn't matter if God Himself told them they were sinners. My mind goes to another elderly Irishwoman I met in rural County Galway, Ireland. Like Mrs. Murphy, she also claimed to have never committed a single sin of any consequence. Standing at her doorstep, I opened my Bible to Romans 3:23, and holding it out for her to read, I quoted the verse: "All have sinned and fall short of the glory of God."

"Paper doesn't refuse ink," she retorted without missing a beat. In other words, you can print what you like, but that doesn't make it so. As she slammed the door in my face, I had a taste of how God must feel when people refuse to accept His written judgment on all mankind—we're all sinners worthy of judgment.

Sacramental Cleansing of Sin

Catholics understand neither their true spiritual condition nor the seriousness of their sins. There are several reasons for this. One is the role baptism plays in Catholic salvation. Administered as soon after birth as practical, the Church teaches that this rite has two powerful effects on a person. First, baptism cleanses the soul of *original sin*, the guilt inherited from Adam. Second, it infuses or pours *sanctifying grace* into the soul. According to the Church, this grace makes the individual holy and acceptable to God. The Church says that through baptism a person is born again, brought into a state of grace, made spotless and innocent before God, and becomes a member of the body of Christ.

None of this is biblical. The Scriptures teach that sinners come into a right relationship with God through personal repentance and faith in Christ (Mark 1:15; Romans 10:9-10). This involves a decision that each person must make for himself (John 1:12-13). Biblical baptism follows as the public expression of one's commitment to Christ as Lord and Savior. It is a symbolic expression of salvation received from Christ, not the means by which we obtain it.

Disregarding Scripture, the Roman Catholic Church teaches that baptism is the *cause* of spiritual rebirth. Parents can and must decide for their children that they will be Christians. And so they bring their infants to the church, the priest baptizes them, and the parish issues a baptismal certificate. These children grow up believing they are right with God and, should they die in a state of grace, heaven-bound. That's why when Catholics like Mrs. Murphy are told that they are lost sinners in need of a Savior, they consider it pure nonsense.

Formalized Excuses for Sin

Another way that Roman Catholicism misleads its people as to their true spiritual condition is by classifying sin into categories. Catholics are told that there are two kinds of sin: *venial* and *mortal*. Most sins are venial, pardonable infractions against God's law, similar to a misdemeanor or a parking ticket. Venial sins weaken a person's spiritual vitality and incur a temporary form of punishment called *temporal punishment*, but they have no ultimate bearing on whether a person goes to heaven or not.

Mortal sins, on the other hand, kill the life of God in a person by removing sanctifying grace from the soul. These serious sins are more like a felony or a moving violation. Should a person die after having committed a mortal sin, he could end up in hell. To be forgiven a mortal sin, a Catholic must confess it in the sacrament of confession (also called the sacrament of penance or the sacrament of reconciliation). This restores him to the life of grace and makes him fit once more for heaven.

According to the Church, however, it's not particularly easy to commit a mortal sin. The Church says that for a sin to be mortal three requirements must be met. First, it must be a big sin, *serious* or *grave* in the vocabulary of the Church. Secondly, the person performing the sin must be conscious that the action is grievously wrong. Finally, the individual must willfully choose to disobey God, though fully aware that God is able to help him resist the temptation.

In practice, these requirements become ready-made excuses for sin. For example, if a man and woman, driven by passions which they feel are beyond their control, fall into sexual immorality, the act, according to the Church, is only a venial sin. In the same manner, Catholics often wink at drunkenness, arguing that a person with a drinking problem may be struggling with a deeply rooted habit, breaking under pressing mental strain, or succumbing to a genetic weakness for alcohol. If committed under such circumstances, not even a lifetime of practicing immorality or drunkenness is punishable by hell. Neither is such conduct a reason to question whether the person is truly born again.

Trivialized Punishment for Sin

Roman Catholicism further misleads its people as to the magnitude of their guilt before God through its teaching that sinners can make up for their sins. The Church says that when a person commits a venial or mortal sin, he stores up *temporal punishment,* which must be paid for either now, here on earth, or later, in purgatory. During his earthly life the person can make restitution for his sins by performing voluntary *acts of penance*, such as abstaining from certain foods, saying series of prayers, offering up his sufferings to God, or giving money to the poor. The individual may choose what form of penance he will perform, or, as is the practice in the sacrament of confession, a priest may assign a specific act of penance. In either case the result is the same—Catholics are left thinking that sin is not that big a deal. How could it be, if saying a few prayers can make up for it?

When I told Tony, an easygoing Catholic, that "the wages of sin is death" (Romans 6:23), he objected, saying, "That's not fair."

"What would be a more just sentence?" I asked.

"Seems like two weeks in hell should be enough," he said, betraying what he thought of his sins and their seriousness before God.

Acts of penance also leave Catholics confused as to the uniqueness and significance of Christ's sufferings on the cross. Pope John Paul II taught that we all share in the redemption through our sufferings.[2] If that's the case, a Catholic might easily reason, "What's so special about Christ's sufferings?"

Ritualized Confession of Sin

Yet another way the Roman Catholic Church misleads people with regard to their sinfulness is by turning confession into a ritual. Priest and parishioner go through a well-rehearsed exchange of responses and prayers. The person lists his sins and their number of occurrences, then says as instructed by the rite, "I am sorry for these sins and all the sins of my whole life, especially for (here he names some particularly grievous sin)." The priest assigns the person a penance and asks him to say an Act of Contrition, a prayer expressing sorrow for sin. He then absolves the person of his sin, supposedly setting him free.

The problem with this ritualized confession of sin is that, like an actor in a morality play, the Catholic has been given his lines. It's all too easy to simply repeat the memorized formula without genuine remorse or intention to change. The person leaves the confessional thinking everything is right between him and God, when in fact he hasn't been talking to God at all.

The most common formula for confession of sin among Catholics is the prayer mentioned above, the Act of Contrition. Many Catholics say it daily, praying:

> O my God, I am heartily sorry for having offended You. And I detest all my sins because of Your just punishment, but most of all because they offend You, my God, who are all good and deserving of all my love. I firmly resolve with the help of Your grace, to confess my sins, to do penance, and to amend my life. Amen.

If said from an informed mind and a sincere heart, the prayer (with the exception of the last line) is biblical and a beautiful expression of sorrow for sin. Rattled off hundreds of times each year, however, it can become meaningless holy poetry. Some Catholics say it multiple times each day.

That appears to have been the case with Mireille, an elderly Catholic woman dying of AIDS. I tried to explain to her that she was a sinner who needed to trust Christ as her Savior. But Mireille just couldn't understand. Whenever we talked about salvation, she would bring the discussion around to her good works and righteousness.

"Have you ever sinned?" I asked her on one occasion, trying to help her see that she was a sinner.

"Yes."

"Have you ever done anything serious enough to send you to hell?"

"No," she replied, calmly shaking her head. She knew herself to be a good Catholic. She had gone to Mass every Sunday for over 60 years, prayed the *Memorare* to Mary, and made an Act of Contrition each day. She had been a good wife and mother, dependable in every way. Even when life dealt her an unfair hand—she had contracted the HIV virus a few years earlier from a tainted blood transfusion—she bore it without complaint.

Admittedly, compared to most people, Mireille was a good woman. She had many admirable traits. But how did her life measure up to God's standard of righteousness as revealed in the Scriptures? That was the issue, not how she compared to other sinners.

On a later visit, with time running out for her, I felt it necessary to press the matter. "Have you ever offended God?" I asked, knowing what her answer would be.

"No."

"Then why do you say the Act of Contrition?"

"What do you mean?" she asked.

"Doesn't it start, 'O my God, I am heartily sorry for having *offended You*'? Why do you pray that if you've never offended God?"

The poor woman had no answer. In her heart Mireille was so convinced that she was a good person, ready to meet God, that my questions made no sense to her. Only God knows if her daily Act of Contrition meant anything. From my conversations with her, I could only conclude that she had repeated the prayer so many times the words had lost their meaning. The prayer continues: "And I detest all my sins because of Your just punishment, but most of all because *they offend You, my God*, who are all good and deserving of all my love." Those are commendable sentiments when spoken from the heart of a truly repentant sinner. But they are meaningless when coming from the lips of a person who actually believes the opposite. Mireille, at least as far as she was concerned, had never offended God. She wasn't heartily sorry. Neither did she detest all her sins. Like many Catholics, she probably didn't even know that the word *contrition* speaks of a deep sense of shame over past sins and a firm resolve to sin no more.

I always marveled how Mireille also denied she had AIDS, despite testing HIV-positive and having every symptom of the disease. Her fingernails were distorted from a fungal infection and her skin scarred where cancerous cells had been removed. Each day her nurses had to swab her mouth with medicine to keep ever-threatening thrush at bay. Once a vibrant woman, she was now a frail invalid, her lungs clogged with pneumonia. Her immune system's T-cell count was 16 (1200 is normal). Yet to the day of her death, she refused to accept her doctors' diagnosis that she was a sick woman with a fatal disease.

It can be the same with Catholics and their sin. Deceived by the lie of self-righteousness, they cannot see their sin despite ample evidence. Sadly, many will understand the magnitude of their guilt only when they stand in judgment, naked and ashamed before God in His holiness. Only then will they know that "all have sinned and fall short of the glory of God" (Romans 3:23).

Deluded as to Their Sins

Being baptized, receiving the sacrament of confession, and saying the Act of Contrition are no substitutes for repenting and trusting Christ to save us. God wants internal, not external brokenness. "Rend your heart and not your garments" (Joel 2:13), says the Lord. David wrote, "A broken and a contrite heart, O God, You will not despise" (Psalm 51:17).

David knew what he was talking about. After he had committed adultery with Bathsheba and had arranged for the murder of her husband, the prophet Nathan rebuked him, saying, "Why have you despised the word of the LORD by doing evil in His sight?" (2 Samuel 12:9). Those words crushed David. In true contrition he cried out to God, writing for all to read,

> Against You, You only, I have sinned
> and done what is evil in Your sight,
> so that You are justified when You speak
> and blameless when You judge (Psalm 51:4).

David allowed God's Word to judge his innermost being. Speaking of the Lord's rebuke, David wrote, "Your arrows have sunk deep into me, and Your hand has pressed down on me" (Psalm 38:2). Overcome by his personal guilt, he confessed his sin directly to God.

> I acknowledged my sin to You,
> and my iniquity I did not hide;
> I said, "I will confess my transgressions to the LORD";
> and You forgave the guilt of my sin (Psalm 32:5).

Unlike David, most Catholics, thinking the majority of their sins have no eternal bearing on their soul, dismiss them as unimportant. I spoke to one Catholic woman in her fifties who was only willing to admit to having committed 20 sins during the span of her life. Others, like Mrs. Murphy, can't recall a single sin. Misled by the Church, these people are deluded, so much so that they can confess each week at Mass that they are unworthy sinners, while still thinking of themselves as good people. The Penitential Rite recited by Catholics at Mass reads:

> I confess to almighty God, and to you, my brothers and sisters, that I have sinned through my own fault (he strikes the breast) in my thoughts and in my words, in what I have done, and in what I have failed to do; and I ask blessed Mary, ever virgin, all the angels and saints, and you, my brothers and sisters, to pray for me to the Lord our God.[3]

At Mass the Sunday before I visited Mrs. Murphy, she had repeated this confession of guilt along with the priest. As she did, she softly struck her breast with her fist as instructed by the liturgy, an expression of the deep sorrow she supposedly felt for her many offenses against God. Just a few days later, however, when I dared to suggest that she was a sinner, she took offense. Ironically, the very passage I asked her to read is the one from which Catholics get the practice of striking the breast when confessing grievous sin. The biblical reference I gave Mrs. Murphy that day was Luke 18:10-14, a parable that Jesus told "to some people who trusted in themselves that they were righteous, and viewed others with contempt" (Luke 18:9).

Two men went up into the temple to pray, one a Pharisee and the other a tax collector. The Pharisee stood and was praying this to himself: "God, I thank You that I am not like other people: swindlers, unjust, adulterers, or even like this tax collector. I fast twice a week; I pay tithes of all that I get." But the tax collector, standing some distance away, was even unwilling to lift up his eyes to heaven, but was beating his breast, saying, "God, be merciful to me, the sinner!" I tell you, this man went to his house justified rather than the other; for everyone who exalts himself will be humbled, but he who humbles himself will be exalted (Luke 18:10-14).

God used this portion of Scripture to help Mrs. Murphy see herself as He saw her. And though at first she took offense—the very thought of her being called a Pharisee!—later she repented, coming to understand the full magnitude of her sin. She trusted Christ and became a sinner saved by grace.

3

Christ Has Done His 99 Percent

Climbing up the steps of the bus that would take me across the width of Ireland from Galway to Dublin, I prayed that God would direct me where to sit. I wasn't disappointed. About halfway to the back of the bus there was an empty seat next to an elderly nun. I sat down and we exchanged names.

Sister Nora sized me up quickly. From my name she knew that I was of Irish descent, and from my accent that I was an American. "Did your parents raise you in the Catholic faith?" she asked in a tone attesting to the fact that she already knew the answer.

"Yes," I responded politely, feeling somewhat as if my second-grade teacher, Sister James Timothy, was about to interrogate me.

"And are you still practicing your faith?"

"No," I told her. "I began reading the Bible several years ago and became a born-again Christian. I left the Church two years later."

Sister Nora frowned. "I don't understand why so many people feel that they have to leave." After a short pause she added, "You should have remained Catholic."

"It was a matter of doctrine," I said. "The Bible teaches that salvation is by grace."

"I believe that," Sister Nora said with conviction. "Salvation is from God. That's what the Church teaches."

"The Bible says 'by grace you have been saved through faith; and that not of yourselves, it is the gift of God,'" I told her, quoting Ephesians 2:8.

"I agree. Salvation is by faith in Christ. Christ died on the cross for our sins. We are saved through Him."

I wasn't expecting Sister Nora's confident replies. She seemed to believe as I did. I decided to test her further.

"Do you think you will go to heaven when you die?"

"Yes. I'm trusting Christ to get me there."

I asked a few more questions and found her every answer "spot on," as the Irish would say. *Maybe she's a believer, a true sister in Christ!* I thought to myself. It's common to hear Christians today claim that there are lots of believers in the Roman Catholic Church. I have met few. The vast majority of Catholics I have spoken to have been depending on a confusing mixture of faith and works to get them to heaven. And up to the time of this bus ride, I had never met a priest or nun who professed faith alone in Christ for salvation. *I guess there's always a first!*

Sister Nora brought the topic back to the Roman Catholic Church. "Read the lives of the saints," she told me. "They'll restore your faith. I'll pray for you."

We chatted much of the way to Dublin. I found Sister Nora, like most nuns, to be a kindhearted woman. And regardless of what Rome taught, I couldn't find anything wrong with her understanding of salvation. Nothing, that is, until we reached Dublin.

"Are you visiting family?" I asked as we pulled into the bus station.

"No, I'm on my way to Rome. The Pope declared this a holy year. Anyone taking a pilgrimage to Rome can earn a plenary indulgence."

The truth comes out! I thought to myself. As we have seen,

Catholicism teaches that every sin incurs a penalty called *temporal punishment*. The sinner must pay this penalty through one of three ways. The first is through suffering here on earth. The second is after death by suffering for sin in purgatory. The third is by obtaining an indulgence from the Church. That was why Sister Nora was on her way to Rome.

Here's how an indulgence works: The Catholic Church claims it is the steward of a vast reservoir of merit earned by Christ, Mary, and the saints. It has the right to dispense credits from this reservoir, called indulgences. These cancel the debt of temporal punishment. A partial indulgence takes away a portion of a person's penalty. A plenary indulgence, like the one Sister Nora was after, cancels all that a person has accumulated up until that time.

The pope, I came to learn, was offering Catholics visiting Rome that year a plenary jubilee indulgence. Pilgrims were required to receive the sacraments of penance and the Eucharist and visit the basilicas of Saint Peter, Saint John Lateran, Saint Paul, and Saint Mary Major. At each location they were required to pray for the pope's intentions (his personal prayer requests). Those Catholics meeting these requirements would receive a complete remission of the temporal punishment for their sins.

"I thought you said Christ died for your sins," I said to Sister Nora, "that salvation was through trusting Him. So why are you seeking an indulgence from the pope?"

"Christ has done His 99 percent," Sister Nora answered. "We have to cooperate by doing our 1 percent." With that she grabbed her bag and disembarked.

Ecumenical Catholicism

Sister Nora had no qualms about adapting the explanation of her Roman Catholic faith for my evangelical ears, a common practice today. Her attitude was, *Our differences are minor, maybe one percent.*

Since we're both Christians, let's emphasize what we hold in common. Hopefully you'll reconsider your decision and return to the Church.

In years gone by, the attitude of a nun encountering an ex-Catholic would have been different. She probably would have refused to talk to me, seeing me as an enemy of the Church, a threat to all that is good and true. But for more than 50 years, the Roman Catholic Church has been taking a conciliatory approach toward non-Catholic Christians. Gone are the anathemas—solemn declarations of excommunication which put critics outside the Church and the salvation it offers. Gone are the dogmatic canons that condemned all teachings contrary to that of Rome. Gone is the haughty arrogance of the Church Triumphant when the pope was carried on a sedan chair by porters and could intimidate kings and emperors.

Picture the winter of 1077. Holy Roman Emperor Henry IV and Pope Gregory VII had locked horns over who held the authority to appoint bishops. The emperor said the pope was a usurper and unfit to rule. The pope said the emperor was an apostate and excommunicated him, placing him outside the Church and releasing Henry's subjects from their oaths of allegiance to him. The German nobles revolted against Henry, and the emperor was left no alternative but to repent. Along with his wife and young son, he sought out the pope, finding him at a castle in Canossa in the mountains of Italy. Dressed as penitents and standing barefoot in January snows, the three begged from outside castle walls for the pope's pardon. The pope left them standing there for three days before finally receiving Henry back into the Church. From then on, "Going to Canossa" became a popular phrase to describe humbling one's self to retain a position.

The days of the Church Triumphant, however, are gone. Having lost most of its ability to terrorize dissenters with threats of spiritual damnation, torture, and execution at the hands of civil collaborators, the Roman Catholic Church has changed its tactics. Rather than calling councils to condemn its critics and their teachings, the Church now chooses to ignore them. The one-time heretics have become the *separated brethren,* for whom the welcome mat is always out. These are wooed rather than warned by the Church. Baptized non-Catholic Christians who decide to formally join the Roman Catholic Church no longer even have to "convert." Now, as fellow Christians, they simply "enter into full communion with the Church of Rome."

The spirit of the day is *ecumenism*—the modern movement seeking to unite Catholics, Orthodox, Protestants, and every other group naming the name of Christ. The "heart of ecumenical thinking," explained Pope John Paul II, borrowing a quote from Pope John XXIII, is that "what separates us as believers in Christ is much less than what unites us."[4] Ecumenism views the differences within Christendom as complementary rather than exclusive. And so, when engaged today in dialogue with non-Catholic Christians, Rome stresses what is held in common. It prefers to blur doctrinal lines rather than delineate them. Every major decision Rome now makes is considered in light of how it will affect future ecclesiastical union. The Church of Rome has committees working for unification with the Orthodox Churches, the Anglican Communion, the Lutheran World Federation, the World Council of Churches, and the World Methodist Council, among others. In the homily of his inaugural Mass, Pope Benedict XVI described ecumenism as a "compelling duty." He said he would "spare no energy" in working to bring Christian churches together. Some Catholic leaders talk of Martin Luther being formally forgiven. Others say the day will come when Rome recognizes Luther as a Catholic saint. Since 1974, when he was the Cardinal Archbishop of Munich, Pope Benedict has been on record as being in favor of the Catholic Church recognizing as consistent with Catholic belief the Augsburg Confession, the first Lutheran confession of faith.

Evangelical Knights

In instances where evangelical Christianity is prospering, Roman Catholicism has adopted evangelical methods to further its goals. A case in point is an advertisement that ran in several American newspapers. It featured a picture of Jesus and a question in large type, asking,

> If You Die Tonight And God Asks,
> "Why Should I Let You Into Heaven?"
> What Will You Answer?

Below, in smaller type, the advertisement continues:

> The answer is looking into your eyes. The answer is Jesus Christ, who died for our sins and rose from the dead to make us God's children. By His grace, we become a "new creation" (2 Corinthians 5:17) and our good deeds become pleasing to God (Revelation 19:8).

What's wrong with that? you ask. Nothing—that's the point! The advertisement's wording, emphasis, and approach are evangelical and biblical. It reads like something out of well-known evangelical James Kennedy's course *Evangelism Explosion*. But it's not. The advertisement's sponsor is the Knights of Columbus, and they are anything but evangelical.

The Knights of Columbus are a Catholic fraternal society claiming 1.6 million members, mostly in North America. Their goals include the expansion of the Roman Catholic Church, promotion of vocations to the Catholic priesthood, greater participation in the sacrament of confession, and the advancement of devotion to Mary. They boast of distributing 100,000 rosaries each year. Since 1947 the Knights have been advertising in secular publications, recruiting for the Catholic Church. At the bottom of the newspaper advertisement described above there was an offer for a free correspondence course called *A Survey of the Catholic Faith,* described as the "basics of Catholic belief, cross-referenced to the *Catechism of the Catholic Church.*"

Now why would a conservatively Catholic group like the Knights want to appear evangelical? Why, in explaining how to get into heaven, is there no mention of the Church, baptism, the sacraments, or the Mass? All of these are necessary for salvation, according to the Church. So are good works. Yet the advertisement would lead the reader to believe that none of these are essential. It presents good works as the fruit, not the root, of salvation. That, however, is the Protestant position—a belief condemned by the Roman Catholic Church at the Council of Trent. Are the Knights of Columbus denying Roman Catholic dogma? Have they switched their allegiance and become Protestants?

Not at all. The Knights have created a clever advertisement that sounds evangelical without compromising a single Roman Catholic belief. They are following the Church's modern strategy in dealing with non-Catholics: Stress what is held in common. The Knights have found that when promoting Catholicism in areas with a Protestant majority, more can be accomplished by taking the profile of the highly successful evangelical movement. The advertisement described above, for example, ran in the *Southern Missouri Shopper,* deep in the Bible Belt of the United States. Generally speaking, the readership would have been wary of anything Catholic. This advertisement, however, would have caught people off guard, and some would have responded.

But don't be fooled by the advertisement. The Knights of Columbus are not about to become Bible-preaching revivalists. The advertisement is evangelical only in appearance. Its wording has been constructed loosely enough to accommodate a Roman Catholic reading. A Catholic theologian might read the Knights' advertisement explaining how to get to heaven in this way (his thoughts enclosed in brackets):

> The answer is Jesus Christ, who died for our sins and rose from the dead to make us God's children [not securing eternal life for those who believe, but opening the gates to heaven, and thus providing the *potential* that some might achieve entry]. By His grace [sanctifying

grace, that is, received through the sacraments of the Church], we become a "new creation" [in the sacrament of baptism] and our good deeds become pleasing to God [earning additional sanctifying grace and eternal life].

Had the Knights' advertisement stated that salvation was *by grace alone through faith alone in Christ alone,* that would have been noteworthy. It would have been a denial of Roman Catholic doctrine, a real turnaround. This would have left no room for the Church's false gospel of salvation *by grace plus merit through faith plus works in Christ plus the Church, the sacraments, and Mary.* The way the advertisement is worded, however, leaves room for both an evangelical and a Roman Catholic reading. This, of course, didn't just happen. The Knights knew exactly what they were doing. Since they began recruiting in secular publications in 1947, more than eight million people have responded to their advertisements, and some 800,000 of these enrolled in courses on the Catholic faith. Whether those responding understood what the Knights were doing is another question.

4

Give Me the Works, Father

From a pew near the front of Saint Julia's Catholic Church, I watched the pallbearers roll Marie's casket slowly down the center aisle. It was a sad occasion. I had known Marie for many years and had tried to share the good news of Jesus Christ with her. I had given her a Bible and had encouraged her to read the Gospel of John.

Marie had said she believed in Christ, but I had my doubts. Not that she didn't believe in Jesus in a historical sense. All Catholics do. What I questioned was whether she had trusted Christ to save her in a personal sense. Whenever I asked Marie about her hope of salvation, she responded with a confused mixture of Christ and self, faith and works, grace and merit. She had never opened the Bible that I gave her. She showed no interest in talking about the Lord. Nevertheless, when a person is dying, friends hope for the best, knowing God to be gracious and merciful.

"Marie wasn't afraid to die," said Father Harry, the parish priest, as he began the eulogy. "I remember how on my last visit to see her, she greeted me as I entered her room. Looking me in the eye, she said, 'I know I'm dying. I have only a short time to live. Give me the works, Father.'"

Marie, in Father Harry's opinion, was a model of how a Christian should face death. I thought the opposite. What little confidence I had that she might personally know Christ vanished with his eulogy. It appeared Marie's dying hope rested in three rituals: confession, communion, and the anointing of the sick—the trilogy of sacraments known as the Last Rites—"the works," as she put it.

Grace Dispensers

Why would a dying Catholic's last request be for a series of rituals? Because Rome has taught its people to approach God not directly, but through a series of rites, the sacraments of the Roman Catholic Church. Catholicism teaches that Christ established seven sacraments: baptism, penance, Eucharist, confirmation, matrimony, holy orders, and anointing of the sick. Each is a channel of a supernatural gift from God called grace. Available because of the merits of Christ, grace is the indispensable and necessary means of salvation and sanctification.

According to the Church, the sacraments dispense two kinds of grace: *sanctifying grace* and *actual grace*. Sanctifying grace gives a person a participation in the divine life of God. Initially poured into a person's soul through the sacrament of baptism, sanctifying grace makes an individual holy and acceptable to God, pleasing in His sight. This grace remains with a person as long as the individual does not commit a mortal sin.

Actual grace is a helping hand from God to do good and avoid evil. It helps a person to perform a specific good deed or act. Because this grace lasts only as long as the situation for which it was provided, the Church teaches that Catholics must be continually obtaining additional actual grace by regularly receiving the sacraments.

In order for a sacrament to effectively dispense grace, the minister conducting it must follow a precisely defined ceremony called a *rite*. Established by the Church, each rite describes the words and actions of both the minister and the participants.

From the Work Performed

According to Catholic theology, the sacraments dispense grace *by the ritual being conducted*. This means that the words and actions of the minister of the sacrament do not merely symbolize or commemorate blessings that the people have already received or are about to receive from God. Rather, the sacrament dispenses grace as the ritual is conducted, "by the very fact of the action's being performed."[5]

This supernatural effect occurs whenever the rite is properly conducted, regardless of the spiritual condition of the deacon, priest, or bishop performing the ritual. In other words, even if the minister is far from God and deep in sin himself, the sacramental rite still produces its intended effect.

How is this doctrine applied in everyday Catholicism? Consider the Catholic archdiocese of Boston. Widespread sexual abuse of children by priests within the diocese were made public through the investigative reporting of the *Boston Globe* in a series of articles beginning January of 2002. The Massachusetts attorney general's office has reported that the abuse spanned not years but six decades, saying, "The mistreatment of children was so massive and so prolonged that it borders on the unbelievable." According to a 76-page report from the attorney general's office, priests have sexually exploited more than 1000 children in the region. One priest, Father John Geoghan, was responsible for abusing more than 130 children.

The Boston scandal unleashed a tsunami that spread across the nation, uncovering similar cases everywhere. More than a thousand clerics have been accused of sexual misconduct. Priests and bishops have been indicted and many convicted of serious crimes. The Catholic Church in America has paid an estimated $1 billion to settle the resulting lawsuits. Boston Archbishop Cardinal Bernard Law, once the most powerful Catholic leader in America, retreated to Rome following calls for his resignation for covering up abuse and shuffling guilty priests from one parish to another.

What is the fallout from these horrific crimes? Many Catholics have left the Church. Others are questioning its veracity as never before. But has anyone challenged the efficacy of the many sacraments performed by the priests now behind prison walls? Have parents inquired whether their children should be rebaptized? Have Catholics who paid for Masses to be said for deceased relatives in purgatory requested a refund? Have those absolved of mortal sins by a sinning priest questioned whether they were restored to a state of grace? Not at all, for as we have seen, Roman Catholicism teaches that sacramental grace is dispensed *from the work performed.* The ability of a rite to confer grace is independent of the spiritual condition of the minister who performs it. Consequently, the Church considers the sacraments administered by these guilty priests equally as valid as if Christ Himself had performed them. Indeed, despite the many accusations against priests in the United States in recent decades, there has yet to be any challenge to the validity of the sacraments that they performed.

One of the most shameless applications of the Roman Catholic belief that the power of the sacrament is in the proper performance of the ritual rather than the spiritual condition of the person performing it (a doctrine known in Latin as *ex opere operato,* meaning "from the work performed") rocked Ireland in November of 1994. A 68-year-old Roman Catholic priest had a heart attack while visiting the Incognito, a gay bathhouse in Dublin that advertises itself as "Ireland's most famous male-only sauna club." Responding to calls for help, two other Catholic priests emerged from private rooms in the club to give the dying man the Last Rites.[6]

One must ask, Is this Christianity? Would the Church have us believe that two men at a gay bathhouse could possibly help a third man dying at that same bathhouse by performing rituals over him? The issue is not whether God is willing to forgive a repentant sinner who cries out with his last breath for Jesus to save him. Rather, the question is, Are Catholic rites so powerful that they can channel God's grace to people even when the priest administering the rite is living an outright lie? And even more to the point, Is Christian salvation and sanctification to be found in rites at all?

The Bible answers no to both of these questions. God is holy. He hates religious hypocrisy. When the people of Israel defiled themselves with the sins of the Canaanites, God told them,

> Bring your worthless offerings no longer,
> incense is an abomination to Me.
> New moon and sabbath, the calling of assemblies—
> I cannot endure iniquity and the solemn assembly.
> I hate your new moon festivals and your appointed feasts,
> they have become a burden to Me;
> I am weary of bearing them (Isaiah 1:13-14).

When the Jews, God's people of the Old Testament, continued in their religious hypocrisy, the Lord proclaimed, "Oh that there were one among you who would shut the gates, that you might not uselessly kindle fire on My altar!" (Malachi 1:10). Likewise, God requires His New Testament people to worship Him "in spirit and truth" (John 4:24). He demands integrity. He desires spiritual worship from obedient hearts.

Yes, God is merciful and He does forgive. But the salvation He offers is not found in rituals, but in a relationship. It's found in a person, His beloved Son. The Scriptures proclaim, "Peace with God through our Lord Jesus Christ" (Romans 5:1). The redeemed are God's adopted children. They have no need for sacraments as a channel of grace. The redeemed have confidence that they stand in God's grace (Romans 5:2). Their access to the Father is through His Son and in the Holy Spirit, not through a priest (Ephesians 2:18).

Mechanical Worship

It's All Planned Out

What has the ritualistic emphasis within Roman Catholicism produced? The result can best be seen in the way Catholics pray. They don't *speak* to God in prayer. Rather, they *say* their prayers, repeating them by rote or reciting them from a book. The Church supplies ready-made prayers for every occasion: for the living, and for the dead; before receiving communion, and after receiving it; morning prayers, evening prayers; before meals, after meals; to confess sin; to honor Mary; and so on. The Church also writes the prayers recited by the priest at Mass. Official liturgy instructs the priest when to kneel, bow, raise his hands, and speak. It tells him what to say and how to say it. The Church strictly forbids innovation, for if the rite is to produce its intended effect, all essential elements of the ritual must be performed precisely as prescribed by the Church.

The Church also scripts the participation of the laity in Sunday worship. The liturgy instructs the congregation when to stand, sit, kneel, cross themselves, and say "Amen." Through a series of rites it guides both people and priest in their Sunday worship: the Introductory Rite, the Liturgy of the Word, the Liturgy of the Eucharist, the Communion Rite, the Concluding Rite.

Not even attendance at Sunday Mass is voluntary. The Church teaches that on "Sundays and other holy days of obligation the faithful are bound to participate in the Mass."[7] The number of holy days of obligation varies from country to country. In the United States there are six. Two honor Christ: Christmas (December 25) and His ascension (40 days after Easter). Three honor Mary: the Solemnity of Mary the Mother of God (January 1), the Assumption of Mary into Heaven (August 15), and the Immaculate Conception of Blessed Mary the Virgin (December 8). One honors the saints: All Saints' Day (November 1). Willing failure to attend Mass on Sunday or a holy day of obligation is a mortal sin.

The effects of this regimented and mandatory worship can be seen in how some Catholics talk about going to Mass. In 1970 the Church began allowing Catholics to fulfill their obligation to attend Mass either on the holy day of obligation or on the evening of the preceding day. Most parishes now offer a "Sunday Vigil Mass" on Saturday evening at 5:00 or 5:30 PM. Well attended, Sunday Mass on Saturday evening is seen as a good way of "getting it over with," as some Catholics put it. Early Sunday morning Masses are popular with the young who don't want Mass to "wreck the whole day." Later Sunday Masses have a reputation of "dragging on forever." They are for the elderly and those who, having been up late the night before, couldn't get out of bed any earlier.

Enough to Fulfill the Obligation

Activity at the back door of the church is also revealing. With attendance mandatory and defiant disobedience a mortal sin, you can be sure that someone has asked, "What if I arrive five minutes late? Is my attendance still valid? And what if I decide to leave early? Have I met my obligation?" Opinion varies among Catholics as to how late one can arrive and still have the Mass "count." Some say you must arrive before the reading of the Gospel, about ten minutes into the Mass. Others say attendance is valid as long as you arrive before the Eucharistic prayer, about 30 minutes into a Sunday Mass. All agree you must remain until the Communion Rite, about seven minutes from the end of Mass.

So what do some Catholics do? They routinely arrive late and leave early. It is not uncommon for some Catholics to walk right out the back door after receiving communion rather than return to their pew for the Concluding Rite. Having punched their spiritual time clock for the week, they leave as soon as legally allowed by the Church. Even Catholics who stay for the whole rite often comment, "I don't get anything out of it." One could only guess what percentage of Catholics would attend Sunday Mass if it wasn't mandatory.

Why Catholics Can't Sing

The detrimental effects of obligatory ritualistic worship can also be seen on the faces of Catholics at Mass. Most, having sat through the ceremony a thousand times, find it hard to keep their minds from drifting. Trying to add some variety to the rite, the Church rotates portions of the liturgy each week according to a liturgical calendar. Following these variations in the printed guides supplied in the pews, however, requires that parishioners flip back and forth between standard and rotated portions—a practice not easily mastered. Most Catholics don't even try, having concluded the benefits are not worth the effort. Only a small portion of the congregation participates in singing the hymns or making the liturgical responses of the Mass. A religious bestseller by Thomas Day, entitled *Why Catholics Can't Sing*, highlighted the widely accepted fact among Catholics that worship at Mass is flat. Day, himself a Catholic, writes: "I would just like to know why congregational singing in Catholic parishes generally does not seem to have any zest at all. Why are all those people staring into space, when they're supposed to be singing?"[8]

In his book, Day cites a University of Notre Dame study of parishes in the United States. Though there were some exceptions, overall, researchers found participation at Mass "mechanical and listless."[9] "Rarely was there an atmosphere of deeply prayerful involvement," reported Mark Searle, one of the authors of the *Notre Dame Study.*[10]

Proponents of the Mass argue that the rite has a solid scriptural basis and that much of the wording of the rite is taken directly from the Bible. They also point out that the Scriptures are read at every Mass. Those who get nothing out of the Mass, they say, have no one to blame but themselves.

The Scriptures, however, have to be used properly if they are to benefit people and engender true worship. This is where the Mass fails. Despite the biblical origins of some of its wording, the liturgy of the Mass is filled with false teaching. And though the Scriptures are read during the Mass—usually a passage from the Old Testament, a selection from the Epistles, and a portion from the Gospels—Catholics don't learn the Bible by attending Mass. Part of the problem is that the Church determines which passages will be read each week, publishing a three-year rotation that chops the Scriptures into bite-size portions.

This all but destroys the context. A short sermon called a homily follows the third reading. It typically consists of 12 minutes of moralizing, storytelling, or fundraising by a priest or deacon. Some priests try to teach the Scriptures, but unsaved and lacking the anointing of the Spirit, they don't understand God's Word themselves. The Bible teaches that "a natural man does not accept the things of the Spirit of God, for they are foolishness to him; and he cannot understand them, because they are spiritually appraised" (1 Corinthians 2:14). Should a priest trust Christ, be born again, and start preaching the truth, the local bishop will soon silence him or force him out.

Impersonal Relationships

The way Catholics interact with one another before and after the Mass also says something about the quality of their worship. They file into church with no more affinity for one another than commuters boarding a train into the city on a snowy February morning. School friends and neighbors may greet each other, but that's the limit.

I remember a weekend when I was still a Catholic that my wife, Jean, and I stayed with Father Barry, a good friend. He was the pastor of three rural parishes, each separated by about an hour's drive. After Sunday morning Mass at the first parish, we traveled with Father Barry to the second so he could say Sunday Mass there. When we arrived, about 30 parishioners were waiting on the steps of the small church. A few greeted Father Barry as he unlocked the church doors and turned on the lights. He then excused himself to put on his vestments for Mass. As we waited for Mass to begin, no one asked Jean or me who we were or why we were visiting their church. Everyone just filed into their pews.

Jean and I were just as bad. Accustomed to the impersonal coldness of our big-city parish, we didn't go out of our way to greet anyone either. Nevertheless, even at the time it seemed odd to us that way out in the countryside Catholics could be so indifferent toward one another. That feeling only intensified when, in the latter part of the

Mass during the Communion Rite, we came to the "sign of peace." That is when, as instructed by the liturgy, Catholics express their unity and love for one another.

His hands extended above the altar, Father Barry proclaimed, "The peace of the Lord be with you always."

"And also with you," we in the congregation answered.

"Let us offer each other the sign of peace," he instructed.

As directed by the liturgy, we each dutifully shook hands with the people around us, offering one another the standard greeting, "Peace be with you."

What did this liturgical greeting signify? Not much. Everyone was simply going through the motions as required by the rite. What did our liturgical worship that day mean to God? Probably not much more. The words of the rite were repeated in the same dull tones to which Catholics everywhere are accustomed. The way we related toward one another as Catholics reflected how we related to God. The Bible teaches that one cannot worship God from the heart and at the same time be coldhearted toward His people: "Whoever loves the Father loves the child born of Him" (1 John 5:1), and again, "The one who loves God should love his brother also" (1 John 4:21).

Talking About Jesus

When Jean and I initially encountered the love that born-again Christians have for one another, it took some getting used to. Not only did the Christians at the first evangelical church we visited greet us warmly, but one family invited us to their home for lunch. Such hospitality was unknown in the Catholicism with which we were familiar.

It also surprised us how many people at that evangelical church returned for the Sunday evening service. Attendance wasn't required; they wanted to be there. When the meeting was over, the people lingered, often for up to an hour, enjoying fellowship with one another. In the weeks that followed I learned that it wasn't unusual for one of the deacons to start flicking the lights on and off to encourage people to leave. "Don't you have homes to go to?" the deacon would tease in a good-hearted way. What a contrast to our parish church, where, following Mass each Sunday, the congregation evacuated as if in a fire drill.

What struck me most about the Christians Jean and I met was the way they spoke about the Lord. They expressed love and appreciation for Him as naturally as they would talk about a member of their family—because He *was* a member. They knew the Lord and loved Him. Their corporate worship was the overflow of that relationship. Reciting prayers was out of the question. All worship was spontaneous, and the singing was heartfelt and enthusiastic. They loved to sing!

By contrast, Catholics seldom talk about the Lord. I remember discussing this with James, a Catholic deacon and graduate of a Catholic seminary. He told me that if someone in one of his theology classes had dared to speak about love for Jesus, he would have been laughed out of the school. Theological, philosophical, social, and political discourse was fine—just don't get personal about Jesus. The same is true of Catholics in general. They will talk about their priest, the pope, religious practices, and moral and social issues. But in all my years as a Catholic, I can't recall anyone initiating a conversation about the Lord. I've never even heard a priest or nun talk about the Lord Jesus in a personal way, with one exception—Sister Brid. For a time she attended a home Bible study I taught. Brid lived in a convent with 28 other nuns. Yet when she wanted to talk about the Lord, she told me, she had to come to our study. In the convent, she said, Jesus' name was never mentioned, except when saying prayers or as part of the liturgy.

It's like that in many Catholic homes. Jesus is a stranger. He lives down the street at the Catholic Church behind the locked doors of the tabernacle on the altar (the small boxlike structure where the consecrated wafers are kept). You genuflect before Him as you approach the altar. You say your prayers to Him. You "believe" in Him. But He is as distant as an uncle in a far-off country—you know, the one you never met. To speak about Jesus with affection around family members would be an embarrassment to all.

Catholics excuse their silence by claiming that their relationship with the Lord is too private to discuss. The fact of the matter, however, is that for most, their relationship with the Lord is too nonexistent to discuss. They don't talk about Him because they have nothing to say.

Much of the blame for this impersonal relationship can be laid at the door of the Roman Catholic Church. It has misled its people, giving them rites instead of a relationship, sacraments instead of a Savior. Consequently, when death draws near, Catholics, like my friend Marie, call not on the Lord to save them, but a priest to give them "the works." In Father Harry's eulogy, he spoke of "the works" but not the *Worker*, the Lord Jesus, who gave His life for us on the cross. There was no reference to Christ's saving work or of God's free offer of eternal life. No, the priest gave Marie what she requested, "the works," and she died peacefully a few days later, thinking she was right with God. As with many Catholics, the sacraments of the Church had lulled her into a false confidence, and she quietly slipped into the next life and the judgment that awaits.

5

Good People Go to Heaven

J essa Vartanian, writing in the *San Jose Mercury News*, described her first visit to an evangelical church as shocking.[11] Though raised with a solid Catholic upbringing, Vartanian stopped going to Mass during her college years, finding it somewhat meaningless. A few years later, sensing a void in her life and looking for spiritual strength, she visited an evangelical church. The minister spoke that day of his mother, describing her as the most loving, caring, and unselfish woman he had ever known. Vartanian recounts, "The whole congregation, including me, was feeling warm and fuzzy." Then, she writes, the preacher "dropped the bombshell." He said, "But my mom isn't going to heaven." Vartanian couldn't believe her ears. "I held my breath," she wrote. "What did he mean? He'd just painted a picture of a saint. Despite being a good person, he said, his mom didn't believe Jesus Christ was her Savior. And, according to him, if you didn't believe that, no matter how wonderful a person you were, you wouldn't be taking the Up escalator."

Vartanian was equally amazed by the reaction of the congregation.

Apparently no one but she was bothered by what the preacher had said. This caused her to question whether Christianity, regardless of the variety, was right for her. Since that time she has developed her own philosophy of life. "What I've come to believe is simple: that if you live a loving, caring life with respect for yourself and others—basically, if you're a good person (and I realize my definition will differ from yours)—that you will 'go to heaven,' or whatever it is that happens when you die, if anything happens at all." Though Jessa Vartanian may not realize it, what she has come to believe has much in common with what she had been taught as a child by the Roman Catholic Church: We are not defiled sinners; sin is not punishable by eternal death; and if you live a good life, you will probably go to heaven.

A Just Reward for His Labors

In Roman Catholicism, entrance into heaven is a merited reward given to those who deserve it. This is expressed throughout the Catholic funeral liturgy. For example, there is a selection of 47 prayers provided to tailor the funeral rite to the particular circumstances of the deceased. These include prayers for a person who has died after a long illness, a person who died suddenly, an elderly person, a young person, a baptized child, and a child who died before baptism. The minister chooses the prewritten prayer that fits best. If the deceased (we'll call him John) happened to have been a Catholic priest, the liturgy instructs the minister conducting the funeral to pray as follows.

> Lord God, you chose our brother John to serve your people as a priest and to share the joys and burdens of their lives. Look with mercy on him and give him the reward of his labors, the fullness of life promised to those who preach your holy Gospel. We ask this through Christ our Lord. Amen.[12]

Notice that this prayer asks God to give the deceased priest what he *deserves:* "the reward of his labors." His recompense for serving as a priest should be "the fullness of life."

If the deceased was an even more deserving person, say a bishop of the Catholic Church, the liturgy instructs the minister to pray as follows.

> Almighty and merciful God, eternal Shepherd of your people, listen to our prayers and grant that your servant John, our bishop, to whom you entrusted the care of this Church, may enter the joy of his eternal Master, there to receive the rich reward of his labors. We ask this through Christ our Lord. Amen.[13]

This is another give-him-what-he-deserves prayer. It asks God to grant the deceased bishop entrance into heaven based on his work. God should give him "the rich reward of his labors." The same kind of prayer is suggested for a pope when he dies. The officiating minister then reads:

> O God, from whom the just receive an unfailing reward, grant that your servant John, our Pope, whom you made vicar of Peter and shepherd of your Church, may rejoice forever in the vision of your glory, for he was a faithful steward here on earth of the mysteries of your forgiveness and grace. We ask this through Christ our Lord. Amen.[14]

This prayer asks God to reward the deceased pope with an eternal "vision of your glory," a reference to seeing God in heaven. The pope should receive this reward, according to the liturgy, because he "was a faithful steward here on earth." In other words, the pope deserves it!

Now what if the deceased were a common man, a real sinner with no personal claim to heavenly reward based on his own merits? The funeral liturgy actually provides a prayer for such a person. It is number 44 in the official Catholic funeral rite. The Church reserves this prayer for a person who committed suicide, which, in Roman

Catholicism, is a potentially mortal sin worthy of hell. Under the Code of Canon Law that was in effect until 1983, a Catholic who committed suicide was denied a Church burial. Since then the Church has taken a more sympathetic view and has lifted the ban. Nevertheless, in the text of the prayer for one who has taken his own life, the Church has little good to say about the person himself. The priest prays:

> God, lover of souls, you hold dear what you have made and spare all things, for they are yours. Look gently on your servant John, and by the blood of the cross forgive his sins and failings.

Amazing! The prayer drops all pretense of deserved reward or personal merit and casts the poor person's soul into the loving hands of God, pleading the only true basis for salvation—the blood of Christ. Unfortunately for the deceased, the Church never told him of salvation through faith in Christ while he was still alive and could benefit from the message. All he heard was that good people go to heaven.

What About Jesus?

But don't Catholics believe in Jesus? Sure they do. The Catholic funeral liturgy mentions Him often. For example, in the opening prayer of the rite, the minister says for the deceased (again we'll call him John),

> O God, glory of believers and life of the just, by the death and resurrection of your Son, we are redeemed: have mercy on your servant John, and make him worthy to share the joys of paradise, for he believed in the resurrection of the dead. We ask this through Christ our Lord.[15]

The liturgy mentions Christ, but it does not present Him as the victorious Savior who died for our sins and offers eternal life to all who trust Him for salvation. Rather, mixed in with grace and mercy, the Church teaches its people that they must merit eternal life. Heaven is the reward for good works and right living. It is for those who deserve it. Yes, Jesus is part of it, but as Rome explains, His death on the cross only made entrance into heaven *possible*. For a person to actually make it to heaven, he must live right and die right. Heaven is a gift and a merited reward for good works performed here on earth.

The result is that when Catholics think about getting to heaven, what mainly goes through their minds is what *they* must do—so much so that some don't include Jesus in their thinking at all. Consider again the 24 Catholics we interviewed outside Saint Patrick's Cathedral. We asked each how they hoped to get into heaven. Only three mentioned Jesus in their answers. Only one of the 24 interviewed made any meaningful reference to Christ's work on the cross. For the rest it was all about what they had to do to get to heaven.

When I told Father Warren, a particularly devout and loyal priest, about the results of our interviews, he strongly protested. "I don't believe it," he said. "The Church teaches salvation through Christ. You can't earn your salvation. It is by the grace of God that we're saved. You might find some poorly taught Catholics who think otherwise, but that's not the teaching of the Church." Admittedly, our sample group in this case was small, but I have found similar results in talking to hundreds of Catholics. The message the people are getting from their Church is that salvation is up to them. Christ has done His part; now they must do theirs. It's Him plus them. Salvation is not through trusting solely in Christ (a belief condemned at the Council of Trent); rather, it is a joint effort of faith plus works. Christ "unlocked the entrance to the heavenly kingdom, which the first man by his sin had locked against himself and all his posterity."[16] That was Christ's contribution. He unlocked the gates. Our part is making it through those open gates. We must do that by living a good life and dying in a state of grace. In the words of the Church, "By His death and Resurrection, Jesus Christ has 'opened' heaven to us....He makes partners in His heavenly glorification those who have believed in Him and remain faithful to His will" (*Catechism of the Catholic Church,* paragraph 18).

Catholic Grace

Father Warren's claim that Catholic salvation is by grace is true, but only to a degree. Roman Catholicism teaches that an unbaptized person cannot earn the *initial* grace of justification. That grace is free, says the Church, being received through the sacrament of baptism. But once in the state of grace, Catholics can and must earn additional grace if they hope to make it to heaven.

Furthermore, what the Catholic Church calls grace is not grace at all. Roman Catholic grace is a thing, something that affixes to the soul. Catholics obtain it initially through baptism. It increases through reception of the Eucharist and other sacraments. It can be earned by performing good works. It can be lost, either partially through *venial sins* (misdemeanors), or completely eradicated by *mortal sins* (felonies). Is this what the Bible means by grace? Not at all. Grace, as Scripture defines it, is the undeserved favor of God toward sinners. It cannot be dispensed through rituals or earned by good works. Neither does God stop acting in grace toward His redeemed children who step out of line. Rather, He disciplines them in love as a father would his children (Hebrews 12:5-11).

Forgetting Jesus

Father Warren was also mistaken in saying that only a poorly instructed Catholic would forget to mention Jesus when asked how to get to heaven. It is often the best-taught Catholics who are most caught up in working for salvation. Father Miguel, a Roman Catholic priest whom we interviewed for the Spanish version of the video *Catholicism: Crisis of Faith* comes to mind. We met him at the Shrine of Our Lady of Fatima, Portugal. He had led a group of pilgrims there from Spain to celebrate the feast of Mary's Assumption. When we asked if he thought he was going to heaven, he smiled widely, swung an arm skyward, and roared, "Of course! I've been a priest for 47 years!"

In his mind, that's all the answer he needed. Mother Teresa of Calcutta may have been equally as confused. She once stated:

> One of the most demanding things for me is traveling everywhere—and with publicity. I have said to Jesus that if I don't go to heaven for anything else, I will be going to heaven for all the traveling with all the publicity, because it has purified me and sacrificed me and made me really ready to go to heaven.[17]

I would like to think that Mother Teresa was being facetious when she made those remarks, but her answer is typically Catholic. I fear that she, like many Catholics, was so wrapped up in her personal works of righteousness that she didn't realize that if she went to heaven there was only one reason: Jesus. Not her. Not Jesus plus her. Jesus alone.

The fact of the matter is that Catholics are not trusting Jesus for salvation. Week after week, from the pulpit and through the liturgy of the Church, they hear a gospel of works. The result is that Christ is not the center of their salvation—*they are.* It's not the poorly taught who believe this. It's Catholics in general.

When I tried to explain this to Father Warren, he wouldn't listen. I finally invited him to join me on the steps of his church the following Sunday. I suggested we survey his parishioners, the Catholics whom he had been teaching. We would determine together who or what they were trusting for their salvation and see how many mentioned Jesus. Father Warren declined the invitation.

A Catholic named Brian was more daring. When he saw our film *Catholicism: Crisis of Faith,* he was so convinced that the interviews outside Saint Patrick's Cathedral had been staged and that the people we spoke to were actors that he decided to do his own survey. For several weeks outside his parish church, as Mass let out from Saint Leander's Catholic Church, San Leandro, California, Brian asked parishioners how they hoped to get to heaven. He was shocked when not one of the 25 people whom he interviewed even mentioned Jesus.

Not easily deterred, Brian waited after Mass the next Sunday and asked the parish priest how he hoped to get to heaven. When even the priest failed to mention Jesus, Brian had had enough. That was the last Sunday either he or his wife, Ana, attended the Catholic Church.

You may want to conduct your own survey. Be careful, though, not to give away the answer in your question. If you ask, "Do you believe Jesus died on the cross for your sins?" expect everyone to answer yes. But if you ask, "How do you hope to get to heaven?" most Catholics will give you a list of activities which they must do. Some will mention Jesus. Some will mention His death on the cross. But don't expect many to say they are trusting Christ alone to save them. That's not Catholic teaching.

6

What Must I Do to Be Saved?

Your question was unfair!" Linda protested. An educated woman in her fifties and a lifelong Catholic, she wasn't about to be proven wrong. I had just shown her a set of illustrated cards, each representing different aspects of Catholic salvation. When I asked her to pick the ones which she thought were necessary to get to heaven, she chose them all. When I asked if there was anything else she needed to do to be saved, she said no. I then pointed out that none of the cards mentioned Christ or His saving work on the cross. That's when she became angry.

"Your question was unfair!" she insisted. "You asked what *I* had to do to be saved. If you had asked about Jesus, I would have"—she stopped mid-sentence, suddenly realizing what she was saying. "I'm sorry," she said in a quieter voice. "I have no excuse. I should have mentioned Jesus. I think I've just learned something very important."

What Linda learned was that Catholic salvation requires a person to do so many things it's all too easy to forget about Jesus. Consider the following question/answer unit from *A Catechism for Adults* by Catholic priest Father William J. Cogan.

Question: What is necessary to be saved?

Answer: You have to be brought into spiritual contact with that saving death of Jesus by faith and Baptism and loyal membership in His Church, by love of God and neighbor proved by obedience to His commandments, by the other Sacraments especially Holy Communion, by prayer and good works and by final perseverance, that is, preserving God's friendship and grace until death.[18]

Note the lack of emphasis on Jesus. The only mention of Him is with reference to being "brought into spiritual contact with that saving death of Jesus." What the catechism means by this is that a person must be baptized. In Catholicism, that's how a person initially receives *sanctifying grace*. This, says the Church, unites a person to Jesus and gives him a participation in the divine life of God. This is just the beginning, however, in the lifelong process of Catholic salvation. Having obtained sanctifying grace through baptism, the Catholic must continue in that grace until death. This is accomplished, as the catechism above states, through faith in God, by loyal membership in the Catholic Church, by loving God and one's neighbor, by keeping the Ten Commandments, receiving the sacraments, praying, doing good works, and ultimately dying in a state of grace. That's a lot to do! Little wonder Linda failed to notice that trusting Jesus as Savior was missing from the set of cards I showed her.

How to Use the Cards

I initially showed Linda nine cards that day. The first eight summarized the Roman Catholic way of salvation and were based on the previously mentioned catechism question/answer interplay. The ninth card was a wild card. I told her it could represent anything she wanted it to. There was a tenth card, which I didn't show Linda until later, which represented the biblical way of salvation—that is, trusting Jesus as Savior.

I designed these cards to help people talk to Catholics about salvation. They have proven to be an effective tool because they provide visual interest, focus the discussion, and help the person see for himself what he is trusting in for salvation. These cards are a tool you can use also.

First, you will need the cards. There's a set of them printed at the back of this book (see appendix A). Cut them out, take them to your local photocopy shop to be laminated, and then keep them at the ready in your wallet or purse. Feel free to make additional sets and share them with your friends. At the website of Good News for Catholics (www.gnfc.org), you can download a free file from which you can print additional sets (these files are available in English and several other languages). There are instructions on the website that tell how to print the cards on ordinary paper or on pre-cut business card forms, such as those available from Avery Office Products.

Each of the ten cards has an illustration on it and a caption at the bottom. They represent the following:

1. Believing and Loving God

2. Being Baptized

3. Going to Mass and Receiving the Sacraments

4. Loving Your Neighbor

5. Obeying the Ten Commandments

6. Doing Good Works

7. Praying and Devotion to Mary

8. Dying with No Unconfessed Mortal Sin

9. Anything Else

10. Trusting Jesus as Savior

The cards are easy to use. You simply present them to a person, explaining each one. You then ask the person to pick up the cards which he thinks are necessary for salvation. Once he has made his selection, review it with him, helping him to see from the Bible what the correct answer is. It's that easy. You'll be surprised how helpful the cards can be when discussing the differences between Catholic and biblical salvation.

The Hidden Card Method

At the risk of turning a simple exercise into an unnecessarily complex one, I want to explain a more effective way of using the cards. You basically use the same approach, with just a few refinements. If you find the Hidden Card Method too complicated, then set it aside and stay with the set of instructions given above. Then after you have gained some experience with the cards, you can come back to this section and give it a second look.

There are seven steps to the Hidden Card Method.

Step 1—Present the First Nine Cards

Begin with casual, everyday conversation. Then move the topic to spiritual matters. When you can smoothly relate the subject to salvation, ask: "Could I show you some cards and get your opinion of them?" Assuming the person agrees (and most will), show the person the cards, saying, "Possibly the most important question in life is, How can I know God and enjoy the next life with Him in heaven forever? These cards represent some of the proposed answers to that question. I'd like to explain them to you, and then ask you which ones you think are necessary to get to heaven."

Lay the first card down and say, "This card represents believing and loving God. Most people think that a right attitude toward God is an important part of getting into heaven."

Give the person a moment to consider the card. Then lay the second card down beside it and continue, "This second card represents baptism. Some people believe you must be baptized in order to go to

Figure 6.1
Present the first nine cards, and keep the tenth card hidden.

heaven. They say baptism removes sin from your soul and makes you right with God." Again give the person a moment to examine the card. Set the third card down and explain, "This card represents going to Mass and receiving the sacraments. Some say this is how we receive the grace necessary for salvation."

Continue to set the remaining cards down one by one, explaining each and giving the person time to consider it before moving on to the next. Here are some sample statements you can use as you introduce the remaining cards.

- ◆ "This fourth card represents loving your neighbor and other acts of charity. This would include obeying the Golden Rule: Do unto others as you would have them do unto you."

- ◆ "This fifth card represents obeying the Ten Commandments. God gave them to Moses on Mount Sinai. Many people believe we must keep them in order to pass the final judgment and get into heaven."

- ◆ "This sixth card represents doing good works. It includes things such as serving our families, giving money to the poor, helping people in need, and doing volunteer work. Some see these as ways to make up for past sins and to earn eternal life."

- ◆ "This seventh card represents prayer and other religious practices, such as devotion to Mary. Some say we should go through Mary to God."

- ◆ "This eighth card expresses the belief that it is the state of your soul at the moment of death that decides your eternal destiny. Even if you were to do all these other things, to go to heaven you must die in a state of grace with no serious unconfessed sins."

- ◆ "This ninth card is a wild card. It can represent anything you want it to. If there's something you believe is necessary to get to heaven that is not represented by any of these other cards, you can make this card represent it."

Do not at this time present the tenth card, "Trusting Jesus as Savior." Leave it in your purse or wallet. Do not let the person see it. You will use it later.

Arrange the nine cards neatly as you lay them out. Three rows with three cards in each row works well. Stress that the cards represent actions that *some* people think are necessary for salvation. You don't want the person to think that you are saying these things are necessary for salvation or that the Catholic Church says they are necessary (which it does). Try to keep the presentation neutral by merely explaining each card without promoting it nor criticizing it.

Step 2—Ask the Person to Select the Cards He Thinks Are Necessary

After you have presented the cards, ask the person to pick up the ones he thinks are necessary for salvation. Frame the question carefully, lest you mislead him. You can say, for example, "Select the cards you think portray what is necessary to get into heaven. Though most of these cards represent good things, I want you to pick up the ones which you think are *essential* for salvation." Give the person a moment to think, then add, "You can pick as many or as few as you think are necessary. You can pick one or all of them. If you think something important is missing, you can make the 'Anything Else' card represent it."

Do not lead the person in his or her selection by your comments or reactions. You want to get a true indication of what the person is trusting in for salvation. You might say, "It's your opinion I want, not what other people think or even what your church teaches."

Once the person has made his selection, verify that he has understood your instructions correctly. Motioning toward his selection, ask, "So you're saying these cards are necessary for salvation? You'd be willing to say to God, 'This is why You should let me into heaven'? Is that correct?"

Then, motioning to the cards the person did not select, say, "And these cards here are not essential for getting into heaven. Is that correct?" You can then move the unselected cards aside. You won't be needing them.

Step 3—Clarify the "Believing and Loving God" and "Anything Else" Cards

Most Catholics choose four to six cards. Some choose all. Selections will vary, but just about everyone chooses the "Believing and Loving God" card. Clarify what that card signifies to the person. You might ask: "What must a person believe about God in order to go to heaven?" A typical Catholic response might be: "You have to believe that God exists, that He's merciful and loving, and that He forgives sin." Others will mention belief in the Trinity, or that God is the Creator. Some will mention Jesus, saying something such as, "You have to believe in the Father, Son, and Holy Spirit, and that Jesus was born of the virgin Mary." A few—surprisingly few—will mention that Jesus died on the cross for their sins. I will explain later what to do should that happen.

Whatever the person says, make careful note of it. This is critical. *You must remember the person's answer for the Hidden Card Method to work.* If you're not sure you will be able to remember, write it down.

Do likewise with the "Anything Else" card if the person selected it. Ask the person what he wants it to represent. Commit his reply to memory or write it down.

Step 4—Help the Person to Evaluate His Selection

Up to this point you have been a neutral observer. You have not offered suggestions or criticized the person's selection. Not wanting to influence their decision, you have not referred to Jesus, the cross, or any of your own beliefs about salvation. But now your role changes. Now your goal is to help the Catholic to evaluate his selection. You are not going to judge it, but help him judge it for himself. You can do this by asking questions that will help him to rethink his choices and compare them with what the Bible teaches.

To illustrate how this is done, we will need to make some assumptions. Let's say your friend chose the first eight cards, a common selection, and one which is consistent with Catholic teaching. Further, let's say that when you asked the person what the "Believing and Loving God" card meant to him, he said, "You have to believe that God is good, that He judges our lives, and that if we confess our sins He will forgive them," another typical answer.

How can you help such a person see that he will never get to heaven the way he is going about it? You will need to show him that 1) he is unable to accomplish the things he believes are necessary for salvation; 2) what he is attempting to do will not make up for his sins; 3) God has provided a better way by which we can be saved—a way that works.

Begin the evaluation process by returning to the first card, "Believing and Loving God." Ask the person: "Are you able to love God as you ought?" Discuss this briefly. Then turn to Luke 10:27 and ask the person to read the first part of the verse. There Jesus teaches, "You shall love the Lord your God with all your heart, and with all your soul, and with all your strength, and with all your mind." Ask the person: "Can you love God as Christ requires?" Hopefully he will see that he cannot.

Next, discuss the three cards that best represent our moral obligations before God. They are the easiest ones to evaluate because they are the hardest to accomplish. These are cards four, five, and six: "Loving Your Neighbor," "Obeying the Ten Commandments," and "Doing Good Works." Though worthy aspirations, who can possibly do these things well enough to get to heaven? Your goal is to help your Catholic friend to see this from Scripture. Ask: "Are you able to love your neighbor the way God expects you to?" Return to Luke 10:27 and ask the person to read the complete verse. It says, "You shall love the Lord your God with all your heart, and with all your soul, and with all your strength, and with all your mind; *and your neighbor as yourself.*" Discuss what this means, and ask the person if he thinks he can love his neighbor as himself. If he tries to minimize this command, have him read the verses that follow. There, Jesus tells the parable of the Good Samaritan. He shows that everyone is our neighbor, and loving our neighbor means meeting their needs. It is a parable well-known to Catholics.

Then go to card five and ask, "Are you able to obey the Ten Commandments to God's standard?" Since you are already in Luke 10, have the person read verses 25 to 28. There, Jesus tells a lawyer who came to test Him that it is possible to get to heaven by keeping the Law, but one would have to actually keep it. Who can do that? Most Catholics will admit they are unable. If the person you are speaking to is like Mrs. Murphy in chapter 2, who believed she had never sinned, you may want to turn to Exodus 20:1-17 and go through each of the Ten Commandments. Point out that the Ten Commandments are not ten suggestions. *Trying* to keep them is not the same as keeping them. Have one or two Bible verses ready to show why no one can get to heaven by keeping the Ten Commandments. A good one is James 2:10: "Whoever keeps the whole law and yet stumbles in one point, he has become guilty of all." Other helpful verses on this point are Galatians 3:10-12, Romans 3:20-28, and Romans 7:7-12. Write these verses on the back of the fifth card to help you remember them. You may also want to show the person the passage I had Mrs. Murphy read, Luke 18:9-14, the parable of the Pharisee and the tax gatherer. Accept the fact that some, as did Mrs. Murphy, will initially take offense. Some Catholics are going to get mad before they get saved. Later they will thank you for having loved them enough to have said something.

Continue with the sixth card, "Doing Good Works." Here you ask, "How many good works must you do to earn eternal life?" Again, help the Catholic to see for himself that he could never do enough good works to get to heaven. Many verses state that salvation is not by works. The best-known one is Ephesians 2:8-9: "For by grace you have been saved through faith; and that not of yourselves, it is the gift of

God; not as a result of works, so that no one may boast." Even our best works are unworthy of God. In the words of Isaiah, "All our righteous deeds are like a filthy garment" (Isaiah 64:6). In this manner, work your way through each of the cards the person selected. Figure 6.2, on page 70, provides questions and biblical references you can use during your discussion.

You don't need to refute every card the person selected. All that is necessary is to demonstrate that the approach the person is taking doesn't work. If he believes *all* the cards he selected are necessary for salvation, then you only have to convince him that he can't do one of them to show his way is doomed to failure. You will find it is surprisingly easy to get most people to admit they can't get to heaven by living a moral life and doing good works. Usually by the time a person has seen he doesn't love God with all his heart, doesn't love his neighbor as himself, and can't keep the Ten Commandments for even a day, the fight is out of him. He's beginning to see himself as God sees him—a sinner unfit for heaven.

Step 5—Present the Problem of Sin

By this point the person should realize he doesn't know how to get to heaven and it's unlikely that he's going there. He's an unworthy sinner. Drive this point home, defining sin directly from the Bible. Two verses you can use are Romans 3:23 and 1 John 3:4. If you have not done so already, review together the Ten Commandments from Exodus 20:1-17. Two passages, both from the Sermon on the Mount, that are especially helpful when speaking to Catholics are Matthew 5:21-22, in which Jesus equates hateful anger with murder, and Matthew 5:27-28, in which He equates lust with adultery. Show the Catholic that his sins reveal what he is like inside—that he, even as you yourself, is a sinner by his very nature (Romans 5:12; Ephesians 2:3). Help him see that his sins are offenses against God (Psalm 51:4; Luke 15:18), and that according to Scripture, the penalty for sin is death, eternal separation from God (Genesis 2:16-17; Romans 6:23;

Card Title	Primary Questions	Helpful Biblical References
1. Believing and Loving God	What must you believe about God? Do you love God as you ought?	Luke 10:27; James 2:19; Matthew 7:21-23
2. Being Baptized	How does baptism help you get to heaven?	1 Corinthians 1:17; Luke 23:40-43; Acts 10:44-48
3. Going to Mass and Receiving the Sacraments	How does going to Mass help you get to heaven? How many sacraments must you receive in order to get there?	Luke 22:19; 1 Corinthians 22:23-26
4. Loving Your Neighbor	Are you able to love your neighbor as you ought?	Luke 10:25-37; 1 John 3:16-18; James 1:27
5. Obeying the Ten Commandments	Are you able to keep the Ten Commandments to God's standard?	Luke 10:25-28; James 2:10; Galatians 3:10-12; Romans 3:20-28; 7:7-12; Luke 18:9-14
6. Doing Good Works	How many good works must you do in order to earn eternal life?	Isaiah 64:6; Romans 3:23; 4:4-5; Ephesians 2:8-9; Titus 3:5
7. Praying and Devotion to Mary	How does prayer help you get to heaven? How can Mary help save you?	Acts 4:12; 1 Timothy 2:5; Ephesians 2:18
8. Dying with No Unconfessed Mortal Sin	How does confessing your sins help you get to heaven?	John 10:28; Romans 5:8-10; 8:33-34; 1 John 5:11-15
9. Anything Else	What does this card represent to you?	John 14:6; Acts 4:12; John 8:24; Matthew 7:13-20

Figure 6.2

Questions and references you can use while discussing the first nine cards.

Revelation 20:11-15). If you sense he is coming under conviction regarding his sin, ask him if he is willing to turn from his sin (Mark 1:15; Acts 3:19).

Step 6—Explain that God's Solution Is Jesus

It's not unusual for a Catholic at this point to say, "If what you've shown me from the Bible is true, then no one is going to heaven!" At this point you've just passed an important milestone. The person, having abandoned all hope of getting to heaven through good works, is beginning to realize the magnitude of his problem and the seriousness of sin. This is a good point at which to respond, "That's right. No one can get to heaven through good works, moral living, and religious practices, because we are all guilty sinners and unfit for heaven. Yet God has provided a solution. Would you like me to show it to you in the Bible?"

Explain God's solution directly from Scripture. Make clear how the Son of God took on human nature so He could represent us before God (John 1:1,14; 1 Timothy 2:5). On the cross, Jesus took the guilt of our sins and paid the penalty that we owed, dying in our place (Mark 10:45; 1 Peter 3:18). His resurrection is proof that His sacrifice was accepted by God the Father as the just payment for sin (Romans 4:25; 1 Corinthians 15:3-4). Show the person that salvation is not a work of man, but of God. We receive it as a free gift through faith (Romans 6:23; Ephesians 2:8-9). Scripture says, "Whoever will call on the name of the Lord will be saved" (Romans 10:13).

Step 7—Encourage the Person to Trust Christ

This final step is when you use the tenth card, "Trusting Jesus as Savior," which you have kept hidden until now. Explain that to receive God's offer of salvation a person must place his faith in Christ to save him (John 3:16; Acts 16:30-31; Romans 10:9-10). This involves a rejection of personal works of righteousness and religious practices for salvation (Romans 10:1-5; Philippians 3:4-11). It is an act of our will whereby we place our faith completely in Jesus to save us. Present the tenth card and say, "This is what the Bible teaches is the way of salvation. It is by trusting Jesus as Savior." Place the tenth card near but separate from the cards the person selected so that he can see the difference. To emphasize the difference, you may want to add, "These are not the same."

Don't be surprised if the person objects, complaining, "But I've always believed that! I believe that Jesus died on the cross for sin." This is another critical point in sharing the gospel with a Catholic. Here you must be firm, look the person in the eye, and state clearly, "No you don't. You haven't been trusting Jesus to save you. Look at the cards you selected when I asked you what you had to do to get to heaven." Help the person understand that you are not saying he doesn't believe in Jesus in an intellectual or historical sense. What you are saying is that he hasn't been trusting in Jesus for his *salvation*. The cards he selected demonstrate this. Remind him what he said when you asked him what the "Believing in God" card represented. This is why you must remember his earlier answer accurately. Help him see that believing that God exists or that God is merciful is not the same as trusting in Jesus for salvation.

Though confronting a person in this way may be difficult, it is the most loving thing you can do. The Roman Catholic way of salvation is a confusing mixture of truth and error. By not allowing the person to escape the fact that he has chosen cards representing a false gospel, you can help him realize for the first time in his life that he is truly lost and needs to trust Christ for salvation.

Encourage the person to trust Christ. Only do so if he is clearly under conviction of sin, repentant, understands the gospel, and wants to follow Christ. Explain to him that he can tell God of his decision directly through prayer. Do not, however, lead the person in a prayer, having him repeat your words after you. Catholicism is an endless series of rites and rituals. Your friend may interpret your invitation to pray to receive Christ as just one more prayer to be repeated. Go slowly. Wait until the person is under conviction of sin and understands the gospel. Then encourage him to make a decision for Christ, speaking to God in his own words. If he is truly ready, he will know what to say.

Outline of the Gospel

An outline of the essential elements of the gospel with Bible verses to support each point is a useful tool for explaining the way of salvation. Here's one you can use when speaking with Catholics.

1. Introduce the Topic

Begin with everyday talk. Then move the conversation to spiritual matters.

Ask yourself: Is the person interested in hearing more?

If the person is interested, ask: Can I show you from the Bible how you can know God as your Father and be certain that you will spend eternity with Him in heaven?

2. Present the Problem

Define sin: Romans 3:23; 1 John 3:4; Exodus 20:1-17; Matthew 5:21-22,27-28

Explain the penalty for sin: Romans 6:23; Revelation 20:11-15

Explain the need to repent: Luke 13:3; Acts 3:19

Ask yourself: Is the person under conviction of sin?

If the person is under conviction, ask: Are you willing to turn from your sin?

3. Explain the Solution

Review who Jesus is: John 1:1,14; 1 Timothy 2:5

Explain what Jesus did on the cross: Mark 10:45; 1 Peter 3:18

Explain that salvation is a free gift of God: Ephesians 2:8-9; Romans 6:23

Ask yourself: Does the person understand the gospel?

If you are unsure, ask the person: Would you explain for me God's offer of salvation in your own words?

4. Encourage the Person to Trust Christ

Explain that salvation is received by faith: John 3:16; Acts 16:30-31; Romans 10:9-10

Ask yourself: Is the person ready to make a decision for Christ?

If the person is ready, ask: Do you want to trust Jesus Christ as your Savior?

What to Do Should the Person Mention Jesus Early in the Presentation

Sometimes when asked to define the "Believing and Loving God" card (Step 3), a Catholic will mention Jesus and His death on the cross. Should that happen, immediately take out the tenth card, "Trusting Jesus as Savior," and present it, saying, "Is this what you mean?" Add the card to the person's selection. Doing so will not make the person's selection correct. Salvation is not through faith in Christ plus obedience to the Law and good works, but through faith alone in Christ. Paul explains this in the book of Galatians. Presenting the tenth card at Step 3 rather than at Step 7 will not ruin the presentation. You may have to adjust what you say, but your presentation can still be effective.

Is the Test Fair?

Some may say the test is unfair. They may say that because you didn't include the "Trusting Jesus as Savior" card in your initial presentation, you misled them. If the tenth card had been presented, they argue, they certainly would have selected it.

Undoubtedly. No one is denying that Catholics believe, at least in an intellectual sense, that Jesus is the Son of God, born of a virgin, that He suffered and died for sin, and rose on the third day. But that's not the point. *The point is that they are not trusting Jesus to save them.*

If the Catholic is trusting Christ for salvation, he has ample opportunity to express it. He could pick the "Believing and Loving God" card, and when asked to explain it, say it represents salvation through believing in Jesus. He might add that he doesn't believe that salvation is through good works, religious practices, or even through loving God. If the "Believing and Loving God" card does not define the matter narrowly enough, he could pick the "Anything Else" card, and only that card. When asked to define it, he could answer, "Jesus," and that would be a perfectly biblical answer.

The test is fair. No true Christian needs a card to remind him that salvation is in Jesus alone. When teaching groups of Christians how to use the cards, I usually begin by testing them as I would a Catholic. Only one person has ever failed the test—a confused Bible college student who, thinking we were role-playing, answered as though he were a Catholic. Try the cards on your Christian friends. You'll see that the test is fair. It is a good measure of what a person is trusting in for salvation.

How You Can Help

1. Catholics are more receptive than most people realize. Each year thousands of them come to Christ. If you want God to use you to help your Catholic friends or family find salvation, make it a matter of daily prayer. Take the initiative to share with them, reaching out in the love of Christ. This is best done in stages, transitioning smoothly from everyday conversation to the important things of life to essential spiritual issues. Here are some questions you can use when the time is right.

   ◆ What do you think it takes to get to heaven?

   ◆ What do you think will happen to you when you die?

   ◆ Can I show you from the Bible how you can have eternal life and *know* that you're going to heaven?

2. When talking with Catholics, try to avoid controversy, comparisons, and criticism. Show the person you really care. You can best do that by being a good listener. And don't be afraid to reach out to priests and nuns. Many are lonely and searching for answers.

3. Many Catholics have a deficient understanding of the seriousness of sin and its consequences. They think that because they have been baptized and are living relatively moral lives, everything is just fine. Help your friend see what God says about sin in the Bible, and pray for genuine conviction. Remember that your Catholic friend's greatest problem is not the Roman Catholic Church, but his sin. So don't let the faults and failures of the Roman Catholic Church become the focus of your discussions. Paul summarized his evangelistic ministry as "solemnly testifying to both Jews and Greeks of repentance toward God and

faith in our Lord Jesus Christ" (Acts 20:21). Do likewise, helping your Catholic friend see that he is a sinner who must be willing to turn from his sin and trust Christ to be saved.

4. When explaining the way of salvation, do so directly from the Scriptures. This will help your Catholic friend see that the authority for what you are saying does not rest with you or with your church, but with God's inspired Word. Make sure he understands what the Bible is saying by asking him to explain it back to you. Since Catholics and non-Catholics use many of the same words but with different meanings, be careful to define your terms.

Part Two

Talking to Catholics About the Mass

7

Is It Really?

As the young priest opened the rectory door, Wilma Sullivan blurted out her request: "Father Phil, I need to talk to you."

"Wilma, I'm awfully busy right now," answered the priest, trying to excuse himself. He knew her well. Wilma was an ex-nun. She had spent four years with the Sisters of Mercy. She attended his church and sang in the choir he directed. He also knew that the young woman could be talkative. "Maybe later. I'm in a rush."

"You've got to talk to me, Father," Wilma pleaded. She paused, gathered her thoughts, and then continued, carefully choosing each word. "I'm trying to salvage my faith. Everything I've believed for 29 years as a Catholic is at stake." With urgency in her voice, she added, "Please help me."

Father Phil knew with a plea like that he couldn't refuse her. "Come on in, Wilma," he said, opening the door fully.

Wilma followed him through the entry hall into an adjoining counseling room. It was arranged much like a small office. He motioned for her to sit and excused himself to notify his housekeeper of the schedule change.

"Now, what's this all about, Wilma?" Father Phil asked as he reentered the room and took a seat across the desk from her.

Wilma noticed him eyeing the Bible she had brought, which was resting in her lap. It made her uncomfortable thinking he might feel threatened by it, but that didn't matter now. "Father, my life's in turmoil," Wilma began in a slow, steady voice. "I need answers."

"I'll do what I can. What's the problem?"

"I'm having terrible doubts."

"About what?"

"Everything! I'm not sure where to begin."

"When did they start?"

"Two weeks ago. I was in the hospital awaiting surgery. A patient from across the hall visited me. Her name was Lenore. She had heard that I was an ex-nun and wanted to meet me. After some friendly conversation, Lenore asked me if I knew what would happen to me if I were to die in surgery."

"Rather brash, wouldn't you say? Some people are absolutely tactless."

"The nurses thought so, too. They shooed her away, afraid she was going to upset me. But you know, Father, it was a good question. I could see she was genuinely concerned for me, and it made me think, *What* would *happen to me if I died?* After we both got out of the hospital, we met and talked more, mostly about religion. I enjoyed the conversation until some of her questions started challenging my beliefs as a Catholic. I finally said, 'Listen, Lenore, I'm a Catholic, and I'm satisfied with my religion.'"

Father Phil applauded. "Good for you, Wilma! None of this surprises me. I've heard it before."

"I did admit to her that I had one question."

"And what's that?"

"It happened while I was still in the convent. I was at Mass, kneeling at the altar rail about to receive communion. The priest came up to me, held the host in front of me, and said, 'The body of Christ.' I knew I was supposed to say, 'Amen,' but I found myself doubting. I was thinking, *Is it really? Is that small bread wafer really Christ?*"

"I don't know if it was wise to tell her that, Wilma. We all experience doubts. It's only natural. Don't let it bother you."

"But that doubt has stayed with me. And that's not all, Father Phil. Lenore began showing me passages from the Bible. For example…" Wilma shifted the Bible in her lap and lifted it onto the desk. It was stuffed with page markers. After checking some of them, she opened to the book of Hebrews, chapter 10. "Father Phil, the Bible says 'we have been sanctified through the offering of the body of Jesus Christ once for all.' A few verses later it says, 'Now where there is forgiveness of these things, there is no longer any offering for sin.'"

"I'm aware of those verses."

"I'm sure I must have read them before, but when Lenore showed them to me I saw something I hadn't seen before. She asked whether I believed the Bible was God's Word. I told her that I did. She said, 'How many times does God say in the Bible that Jesus had to be offered for sin?' I told her we had just read it: 'once for all.' I said, 'Lenore, what's wrong with that?' She said, 'How many times does your Church offer Christ for sin?' Father Phil, I was about to say, 'Every day at Mass,' when it struck me that that contradicted the Bible. I didn't know what to say. I just looked at her with my mouth open."

"She was trying to confuse you, Wilma. I've run into people like her before. Don't pay any attention."

"Lenore said, 'Wilma, they're different, aren't they? What your Church says and what the Bible says.' I didn't know how to answer her. Then she said to me, 'So who are you going to trust? God, who cannot lie to you in the Bible, or men, who can make mistakes?' Father Phil, that was only the beginning." For the next 45 minutes, Wilma recounted how Lenore and she had met almost daily for the past two weeks, studying the Bible and talking about what it said. Wilma had also visited Lenore's church and met her pastor. She reviewed with Father Phil their discussions on worship, devotion to Mary, the sacraments, purgatory, baptism, and the way of salvation. The priest listened without comment as Wilma became more impassioned with each new topic.

"Father Phil," Wilma told the priest, "what Lenore was showing me from the Bible made a lot of sense. I found the Bible, my *Catholic Bible,* saying one thing and the Church saying something else. Father Phil, the Bible says—"

"I don't care what the Bible says," the priest finally interrupted. "The Church doesn't depend solely on what the Bible says for her doctrine. We have Tradition. You of all people, Wilma, should know that. If your reading of the Bible doesn't line up with the Church's teaching, you know what you need to do: Put down your Bible and do what the Church tells you. That's why we have the Church."

"But Father Phil, these matters are substantial. I can't just ignore the Scriptures." She was now more agitated than ever. She paused to calm herself, then added, "I'm thinking of leaving the Church."

"Wilma! You'll never leave the Catholic Church."

"I've been here for almost an hour, Father Phil. You've no answers for my questions. How can you tell me I'll never leave?"

"You're too steeped in Tradition. You'll never leave. Never!"

Bound to the Church

The Mass is one of the most powerful forces binding Catholics to the Church of Rome. The Second Vatican Council described the Mass as "the source and summit of the whole Christian life,"[19] "the greatest gift of all."[20] It is the focal point of Catholic liturgy. Everything within Catholicism revolves around it. It is the primary point of contact between Catholics and the Church, and the chief way in which the Catholic faith is handed down from one generation to the next. More than any other single thing, the Mass is Roman Catholicism.

Attendance, for Catholics, is mandatory. The Church mandates that all Catholics must attend weekly. It recognizes "legitimate" reasons for failing to meet this "holy obligation," such as illness, caring for a sick child or parent, or the inability to get to church while traveling. But deliberate disobedience is a mortal sin, punishable by hell. To be forgiven, a Catholic must confess to a priest, in the sacrament of penance, how many times he missed Mass.

The Church teaches that Catholics are not only morally obliged to go to Mass, but dependent upon it for salvation. This is because of a miraculous event that allegedly occurs at every Mass. During the part of the Mass called the consecration, the Church teaches that the bread and wine turn into the actual body and blood of Jesus. Christ comes to exist, says the Church, in His full deity and humanity under the appearances of bread and wine.

In acknowledgment of this supposed miraculous change, the Church instructs its people to kneel at the moment of consecration and adore the transformed bread and wine. They are to direct their praise, worship, and thanksgiving to it. For this reason, Catholics also refer to the consecrated bread and wine as the *Eucharist*, from the Greek word for *thanksgiving*.

Following the consecration is the Communion Rite. This is when Catholics leave their pews, go to the front of the church, and receive the Eucharist—usually just the bread, sometimes the bread and the wine. The Church teaches that in this rite, Catholics are receiving Christ's body and blood. This unites them more closely with God. The Eucharist, says the Church, is spiritual food for the soul. It nourishes, strengthens, and revives those participating in the Mass, especially those who receive communion.

These benefits, says the Church, are produced because the Eucharist is a source of grace, one of the seven sacraments of the Roman Catholic Church. It is the *Blessed Sacrament*, the primary and most sacred channel of grace to Catholics. Through it Catholics receive the grace they need to make it to heaven: sanctifying grace to make them holier and more acceptable to God, and actual grace to help them do good works and avoid evil.

Roman Catholicism also teaches that the Mass is an actual sacrifice for sin, the continuation of the sacrifice that took place on the cross. At the consecration of the Mass, Christ comes to exist upon the altar in His victimhood. There He experiences an "unbloody immolation," in which the priest offers Christ as a living sacrifice. This occurs during the Mass as the priest prays,

> Father, calling to mind the death your Son endured for our salvation, His glorious resurrection and ascension into heaven, and ready to greet Him when He comes again, we offer you in thanksgiving this holy and living sacrifice. Look with favor on your Church's offering, and see the Victim whose death has reconciled us to yourself.[21]

Roman Catholicism teaches that this offering of the Eucharist *presents again* the sacrifice of the cross to God the Father. It soothes the wrath of God, making reparation for the sins of the living and the dead, and applies the saving power of the cross to Catholics.

These beliefs about the Mass bind Catholics to the Church. It teaches them from childhood that only through the Mass can they experience the material presence of Christ, worship Him under the appearances of bread and wine, and receive Him into themselves in holy communion. Only through the sacrament of the Eucharist can they receive the grace necessary for salvation. And only through the sacrifice of the Mass can they participate in Christ's offering, making satisfaction for their sins and those of their loved ones in purgatory, thereby speeding their release. For these reasons, Catholics stand in awe of the Mass, revering it above all other religious practices.

For Catholics the Mass has a magical, almost eerie feel to it. A ritual so shrouded in mystery that no one can adequately explain it, Rome's theologians call it a "mystical reality." Adding to its otherworldly quality are the liturgy, vestments, altar, candles, and music. The result is that most Catholics consider the Mass beyond scrutiny. Anyone so bold as to question its validity would surely be guilty of blasphemy.

These doctrines concerning the Mass are an important part of the reason Father Phil was so confident that Wilma Sullivan would never leave the Church. In his words, she was "too steeped in Tradition" to ever leave. Father Phil, however, was unaware that Lenore was not the only one raising questions in Wilma's mind about the Mass. The Spirit of God was also speaking to her and bringing her to the one who promised, "You will know the truth, and the truth will make you free" (John 8:32). Wilma was about to be set free.

Is the Eucharist Really Christ?

When the priest held the consecrated wafer in front of Wilma Sullivan and said, "The body of Christ," she found herself wondering, *Is it really?* The Mass, and Roman Catholicism with it, stands or falls on that question.

Is the Eucharist the real body of Christ? The Roman Catholic Church answers yes. "In the most blessed sacrament of the Eucharist 'the body and blood, together with the soul and divinity, of our Lord Jesus Christ and, therefore, *the whole Christ is truly, really, and substantially* contained.'"[22] The Church bases this belief on John chapter 6. There Jesus taught,

> I am the living bread that came down out of heaven; if anyone eats of this bread, he will live forever; and the bread also which I shall give for the life of the world is My flesh....Truly, truly, I say to you, unless you eat the flesh of the Son of Man and drink His blood, you have no life in yourselves. He who eats My flesh and drinks My blood has eternal life, and I will raise him up on the last day. For My flesh is true food, and My blood is true drink (verses 51-55).

Here, according to the Church, Jesus is "urging us to receive Him in the sacrament of the Eucharist."[23] He is promising that He will give His flesh for us to eat as a life-giving sacrament of the Church. This is the Roman Catholic interpretation of John 6.

The context of the chapter, however, does not support this Catholic interpretation. The passage is not about sacraments, but about Jesus Himself and the necessity of personal faith in Him for salvation. In John 6 Jesus teaches,

> This is the work of God, that you believe in Him whom He has sent....For this is the will of My Father, that everyone who beholds the Son and believes in Him will have eternal life; and I Myself will raise him up on the last day....Truly, truly, I say to you, he who believes has eternal life (verses 29,40,47).

Here Jesus is teaching that to enjoy the next life in heaven, a person must fully trust Him as Savior. In order to illustrate this important truth, the Lord uses an analogy in which He compares the necessity of eating bread for physical life with the necessity of believing in Him for spiritual life.

> I am the bread of life; he who comes to Me will not hunger, and he who believes in Me will never thirst....I am the living bread that came down out of heaven; if anyone eats of this bread, he will live forever; and the bread also which I will give for the life of the world is My flesh (verses 35,51).

When Christ speaks here of giving His flesh for the life of the world, He is referring to the shedding of His blood on the cross for our sins. There is nothing in the context to suggest a liturgical rite such as the sacrament of the Eucharist is what is intended.

John 6 explains itself, as any objective person reading it quickly realizes. Being objective about John 6, however, is difficult for Catholics. Having been taught all their lives that the chapter is speaking of the Eucharist, it is nearly impossible for them to see it any other way.

I know this from personal experience. Two years before I left the Catholic Church I began studying the Bible. After much time I came to realize that John 6 was talking about faith in Christ, not the Eucharist. But only after I had been out of the Catholic Church ten years was I able to see that Jesus isn't talking about actual bread in John 6. He doesn't even mention wine. The passage isn't about the Last Supper (the meal shared by Christ and His disciples on the night of His betrayal) or the Lord's Supper (the memorial feast observed by Christians since the first century). The context is completely different. It took ten years of separation from the Roman Catholic Church before I could see this. Since then I have tried to help others to understand John 6. I have found that those still in the Church find it almost impossible to interpret the chapter objectively.

Stephen, a well-informed and articulate Catholic, was one such person. We exchanged numerous lengthy letters about the Mass. I tried to help Stephen to see that Jesus is making a comparison in that chapter. Just as the Jews were dependent upon manna for physical life in the wilderness, so we are dependent upon Jesus for spiritual life. He is the "bread of life" (John 6:35) who "comes down out of heaven, and gives life to the world" (John 6:33). I explained to Stephen how the parallel structures of John 6:40 and John 6:54 demonstrate that when Jesus refers to the eating of His flesh He is illustrating the need for complete trust in Him for salvation. He isn't talking about real bread or anyone actually eating His flesh. Yet Stephen could only see the passage the Roman Catholic way.

Catholics find the Gospel accounts of the Last Supper almost as difficult to understand clearly. The Scriptures tell how Jesus, taking bread and blessing it, broke it and gave it to His disciples, saying, "This is My body" (Matthew 26:26). Likewise, He took a cup of wine, saying, "This is My blood" (Matthew 26:28). The Roman Catholic Church says that with those words the Lord miraculously transformed the bread and wine into His actual body and blood. He then offered them to God as a sacrifice for sin. This, according to the Church, not only symbolized what would happen the next day on Calvary, but made the yet-future sacrifice of the cross "really present"[24] at the Last Supper. Christ then gave His flesh and blood to His disciples to eat and drink. This, says the Church, was the fulfillment of Jesus' promise in John 6. And so at every Mass the liturgy of the Church instructs the priest to take the bread, hold it above the altar, and pray, "Blessed are you, Lord, God of all creation. Through your goodness we have this bread to offer which earth has given and human hands have made. It will become for us the bread of life."[25] Moments later the priest offers a similar prayer to God: "Bless and approve our offering; make it acceptable to you, an offering in spirit and in truth. Let it become for us the body and blood of Jesus Christ, your only Son, our Lord."[26]

The Lord Jesus never said, however, that the bread and wine would *become* His body and blood. What He said was "This *is* My body" (Matthew 26:26) and "This *is* My blood" (Matthew 26:28). The most natural reading of the text is that at the Last Supper Jesus used bread to represent His body and wine to represent His blood. He meant for His words to be taken in their figurative sense.

Transubstantiation

Even the most zealous proponents of the Mass must concede that the bread and wine look suspiciously alike before and after the consecration. Nothing happens. Of course, the Church has an answer. It says the change cannot be seen because the bread and wine are transformed internally, not externally. More precisely, they do not undergo a transformation, but a *transubstantiation*, a term rooted in an ancient and obsolete metaphysical concept of nature put forth by Aristotle. He theorized that all matter consisted of two parts: *accidents* and *substance*. Accidents, said Aristotle, are the outward appearance of matter (how it looks). Substance is its inner essence (what it is). Today we know that the way something looks is determined by the molecular structure of the material or what it is. Regardless, in explaining the "miraculous" change of the bread and wine, the Church adapts Aristotle's concept of matter and says the inner substances of the bread and wine cease to exist. All that remains is their outward appearance. Though both objects continue to look, feel, smell, and taste like bread and wine, they have nevertheless profoundly changed. By the miracle of transubstantiation, their inner natures have ceased to exist and have been replaced by the substance of Christ's body and blood. Christ, says the Church, becomes present "in the fullest sense,"[27] the "true body of Christ the Lord, the same that was born of the Virgin."[28]

The Church calls this manifestation of Christ in the consecrated bread and wine the *real presence*. What is *real* about it, however, is difficult to understand, for the Church has defined a new mode of existence known neither to Aristotle, modern science, or the Bible. Even the Church admits this new mode of existence is "altogether unique."[29] What occurs, says the Church, "cannot be apprehended by the senses,"[30] for it "defies the powers of conception."[31] Ironically, in explaining why the change cannot be observed, the Church employs the teaching of Aristotle, honored by historians as the father of empirical science, which deals with knowledge gained through observation and experimentation rather than philosophical theory. Understandably, many modern Catholics find the theory of transubstantiation hard to accept, if not absolute nonsense. A 1992 Gallup poll in America reported that "less than a third of Roman Catholics believe that when they receive communion at Mass they receive the body and blood of Jesus Christ in precisely the way the Church teaches."[32] A graduate of a Jesuit seminary told me that none of his professors believed in transubstantiation as an explanation of what takes place at Mass.

Although many Catholics doubt the Church's explanation as to how the bread and wine change, most believe that they do, nevertheless, change. After three decades of decline, the worship of the Eucharist as divine is now on the increase, both during the Mass and on special occasions, such as the Exposition of the Blessed Sacrament. That is when a priest inserts a large consecrated wafer into a glass receptacle and mounts it in a *monstrance*—a gold stand usually resembling a sunburst—and places it on an altar. Catholics assemble to worship the host by the hour. In the Perpetual Adoration of the Blessed Sacrament, Catholics take turns day and night in uninterrupted worship of the consecrated bread wafer. The Church has authorized the formation of several religious orders in which members dedicate their lives to this purpose, worshiping the host in shifts around the clock. There are accounts of unbroken worship of the Eucharist spanning not just years but centuries. The continuous adoration of the Blessed Sacrament by Catholics at the Cathedral of Lugo, Spain, is said to have exceeded 1000 years. Some Catholics spend several hours each week bowed in adoration before a consecrated bread wafer. Such was the practice of Mother Teresa of Calcutta during her lifetime. She said, "I make a holy hour each day in the presence of Jesus in the Blessed Sacrament. All my sisters make holy hours as well."[33]

The sincerity of Catholics in following their Church's instruction to worship the Eucharist must be acknowledged. The practice is nevertheless idolatrous. The Ten Commandments forbid the worship of any object, even those supposedly representative of God (Exodus 20:4-5). God has told us that He will never inhabit an object so as to be worshiped: "I am the LORD, that is My name; I will not give My glory to another, nor My praise to graven images" (Isaiah 42:8). Jesus taught, "God is spirit, and those who worship Him must worship in spirit and truth" (John 4:24).

Liberating Truth

Liberation came for Wilma Sullivan one Sunday a few weeks after her visit with Father Phil. As she drove to church, her soul was in torment, struggling to reconcile what she had been learning from the Bible with her Catholic faith. Tears began trickling down her cheeks. She finally cried out, "God, You've got to straighten this out. I'm so confused!"

Arriving at her parish church, Wilma took a seat high in the choir loft at the rear of the building. From there she watched as the priest performed the same familiar ritual she had seen a thousand times. This time, however, something unusual happened. At the consecration of the bread, the priest elevated the host, saying, "Take this, all of you, and eat it: This is my body which will be given up for you." As he did, from Wilma's vantage point high in the choir loft at the rear of the church, she found herself looking over the top of the wafer into the eyes of a figure of Jesus hanging on a large crucifix behind the altar. At the moment the priest said, "This is my body," a phrase from Scripture went through her mind: "once for all." Wilma felt as though the Lord were saying to her, *Wilma, I died once for all. I don't need to be on this cross. I don't need to be in this host.* The same thing happened a moment later when the priest raised the chalice, saying, "Take this, all of you, and drink from it: This is the cup of my blood, the blood of the new and everlasting covenant. It will be shed for you and for all men so that sins may be forgiven." *No, Wilma,* she sensed the Lord saying to her. *I died once for all.*

Wilma was set free at that Mass. With God's help she left the Catholic Church, never attending Mass again as a Roman Catholic or receiving the Eucharist.

Symbols of Christ's Body and Blood

At the Last Supper, Jesus used bread and wine as symbols of His body and blood. As the following points explain, this is how Jesus intended for us to view them.

- Nothing in the Gospel accounts of the Last Supper indicate that the bread and wine changed or that those present worshiped them as divine. If this had been so, it certainly would have been mentioned in all accounts of the Last Supper.

- No reasonable person present at the Last Supper would have taken Jesus' words to mean that He was both at the table and on the table and later under the table as crumbs were scattered.

- The Lord frequently used figurative language in His teaching, even using the same verb translated "is" in His words "This is My body" (see John 6:48; 8:12; 10:9,11; 11:25; 14:6; 15:1).

- At the conclusion of the Last Supper, Jesus told His disciples, "These things I have spoken to you in figurative language" (John 16:25).

- The Lord said of the wine, "This is My blood" (Matthew 26:28). If these words had changed the wine into His blood, Jesus would not have still referred to it as wine a moment later, saying, "I will not drink of *this fruit of the vine* from now on until that day when I drink it new with you in My Father's kingdom" (Matthew 26:29, emphasis added).

- Nothing in the book of Acts indicates that the first Christians believed the bread and wine changed. Neither do the epistles speak of such a change.

- The Roman Catholic interpretation requires the eating of human flesh and drinking of human blood. This is strictly forbidden by Scripture (Leviticus 17:10-14; Acts 15:29).

- Scripture never ascribes more than one location at any given time to Christ's bodily presence. According to the Bible, He is now enthroned in heaven. Christians are awaiting His second coming. He cannot, therefore, be bodily present in thousands of Catholic churches around the world as Rome claims.

- There is no precedent in Scripture for a miracle in which God expects the faithful to believe that something supernatural has occurred when all outward evidence indicates that nothing has occurred. (Does the fable of the emperor's new clothes comes to mind?)

8

I Never Heard That at Mass

I met Anthony through his sister, Teresa. She had come to know Christ several years earlier and had left the Catholic Church. She had been sharing the gospel with Anthony, and he, too, now claimed to be a born-again Christian. Yet he remained loyal to the Catholic Church and its practices, attending Mass each week and teaching catechism in his parish.

"How can you say what Christ did on the cross can save you," I asked him, "and still attend Mass?"

"What's the problem?" he asked.

"It's a sacrifice," I said. "An ongoing sacrifice for the sins of the living and the dead."

"No it's not," Anthony said.

I showed him the eucharistic prayer from the liturgy of the Mass. "What does the priest pray after consecrating the bread and wine?" I asked.

Anthony read the prayer. "We offer to you, God of glory and majesty, this holy and perfect sacrifice, the bread of life and the cup of eternal salvation."[34] He paused, then said, "I don't recall the priest saying that."

"Read at the next section," I said.

"Look with favor on these offerings," Anthony read, "and accept them as once you accepted the gifts of your servant Abel, the sacrifice of Abraham, our Father in faith, and the bread and wine offered by your priest Melchizedek. Almighty God, we pray that your angel may take this sacrifice to your altar in heaven. Then, as we receive from this altar the sacred body and blood of your Son, let us be filled with every grace and blessing." Anthony studied the prayer for a few moments, then added, "I never heard that at Mass." Having attended for more than 40 years, he was certain that he was right.

"I'm not making this up," I told him. "Next Sunday sit near the front and listen to the words of the priest. You'll see for yourself."

What Anthony Didn't Know

Apparently Anthony didn't know that one of the main purposes of the Catholic priesthood is to perpetuate the sacrifice of the cross through the Mass. At every Mass, through the consecration of bread and wine, the priest supposedly presents Christ in His victimhood. This is portrayed through the separate consecration of the bread and wine, Christ's body in the hands of the priest holding the wafer, Christ's blood in the chalice (the cup-shaped goblet used by the priest), His body and blood separated, a picture of death. That weekly imagery of what the Church considers a reality had been lost on Anthony. Somehow he had never heard the priest pray over the consecrated bread and wine, "Look with favor on your Church's offering, and see the Victim whose death has reconciled us to yourself."[35] He didn't know that each offering of the Mass re-presents Christ to the Father. According to the Church, it is an unbloody sacrifice that atones for the sins of the living and the dead by appeasing the wrath of God. Neither had it occurred to Anthony that the consecrated wafer is called a *host* because Christ is the Victim of the Mass, the word *host* coming from the Latin *hostia*, meaning "sacrificial victim."

Somehow Anthony had missed all of this. He hadn't noticed that the priest stood not at a table, as was used by Christ at the Last Supper, but at an altar, a raised structure designed for sacrifice. Somehow he had missed that, though an altar is the centerpiece of every Catholic church. That being the case, it is unlikely that Anthony knew anything about how the altar had been dedicated for sacrifice. Church law requires that a solemn rite be performed in which relics are placed within a small cavity at the front of every non-movable altar. [36] This cavity is called the *sepulcher,* and canon law states that it must contain relics such as a finger bone, a tongue, or some dried blood in a glass vial. These must be of such size that they can be easily recognized as human body parts and have been officially authenticated by the Church as having come from the cadaver of a Catholic martyr or saint. A flat stone, called an *altar stone,* covers the sepulcher and constitutes the "altar proper," the spot where the bread and wine are to be placed during the Sacrifice of the Mass.

Had Anthony known these things, he may have seen the Mass differently, but then again, maybe not. Anthony was a loyal Roman Catholic. He was convinced that the Church could not possibly be wrong about such things. Now, if it had been another Christian church doing these things, well, that might have been another story. If, for example, it had been his sister's evangelical church that had dug up one of their deceased pastors, cut off his left thumb, placed it in a glass receptacle, and put it on the table where they celebrated the Lord's Supper each Sunday, he probably would have labeled them a cult. For the Catholic Church to do such a thing, however, was somehow different. Catholics typically reason that if it comes from the ancient Church instituted by Christ, it could hardly be wrong.

And so Anthony continued to attend Mass each week, unaware of what was really taking place on the altar, unaware that he was not only attending but participating in the sacrifice of Christ. Each week the priest, speaking on behalf of those present, prayed, "We offer you His body and blood, the acceptable sacrifice which brings salvation to the whole world."[37] And each week, though he did not realize it, Anthony was offering Christ as a sacrifice along with the priest. The Church states, according to the Second Vatican Council:

> It is indeed the priest alone, who, acting in the person of Christ, consecrates the bread and wine, but the role of the faithful in the Eucharist is to recall the passion, resurrection and glorification of the Lord, to give thanks to God, and to offer the immaculate victim not only through the hands of the priest, *but also together with him*; and finally, by receiving the Body of the Lord, to perfect that communion with God and among themselves which should be the product of participation in the sacrifice of the Mass (emphasis added).[38]

Had Anthony known the Mass was a sacrifice and that he was offering it along with the priest, he may have asked: *Why would we want to continue the crucifixion of Christ?* Surely he knew that the crucifixion of Christ was a horrific event of unimaginable cruelty. Surely he knew that it was Christ's enemies who had crucified Him, not His disciples who loved Him. Surely if Anthony had known that the Mass was a sacrifice and that he was expected to offer it with the priest he would have objected. But then again, maybe not, for Anthony, having only a cursory knowledge of Scripture, would not have known how biblically wrong it would be for a Christian to participate in such a sacrifice.

Is Anything Sacred?

Anthony probably didn't know that the Old Testament solemnly warns against unauthorized sacrifice (Exodus 22:20; Deuteronomy 13:6-11). He probably didn't know that according to the Hebrew Scriptures the placement of human body parts in an altar would defile it, not sanctify it, and make it ceremonially unclean. Under Jewish law, anyone who touched a corpse was "unclean for seven days" (Numbers

19:11). Coming in contact with a human bone or a grave also defiled a person (Numbers 19:16). The law of Moses specifically forbade the Jewish priests from contact with the dead (Leviticus 21:1-12). When King Josiah wanted to defile the unauthorized altar of Israel at Bethel, he did so by burning human bones on it (2 Kings 23:16).

Anthony also probably didn't know that as Jesus died He cried, "It is finished!" (John 19:30). Anthony may have never heard Jesus' last words, for somehow John 19:30 hadn't made it into the three-year cycle of Scripture readings at Mass.

Yet other Scriptures just as clear did make it into the rotation. Many of the clearest statements are from Hebrews chapters 9 and 10. There we read that Christ died "once for all" (Hebrews 9:12,26,28; 10:10). He "entered the holy place once for all, having obtained eternal redemption" (Hebrews 9:12). He, "having offered one sacrifice for sins for all time, sat down at the right hand of God, waiting from that time onward until His enemies be made a footstool for His feet. For by one offering He has perfected for all time those who are sanctified" (Hebrews 10:12-14). "There is no longer any offering for sin" (Hebrews 10:18). But if after attending Mass for 40 years Anthony hadn't even realized the priest was offering a sacrifice, it is unlikely he would have realized the significance of Hebrews 9–10. And even if he had, he wouldn't have applied them in a critical way to a practice of the Church, for in Roman Catholicism, Church dogma and Church practice determine the meaning of the Scriptures, not the other way around. Theologians and priests are obliged to interpret the Bible in the sense that has been assigned to it by the Church. Consequently, the Bible always agrees with the Church—even when it doesn't.

Case in point: Pope John Paul II's explanation of the Mass in his bestselling book *Crossing the Threshold of Hope.* There he wrote,

> The Church is the instrument of man's salvation. It both contains and continually draws upon the mystery of Christ's redemptive sacrifice. Through the shedding of

His own blood, Jesus Christ constantly "enters into
God's sanctuary thus obtaining eternal redemption" (cf.
Hebrews 9:12).[39]

*Here Pope John Paul II actually altered Hebrews 9:12 to make it agree
with Roman Catholic doctrine.* Three changes are apparent which so
distort the meaning of Scripture that the former pope's version actually communicates the very opposite of the original text. Before we
look at those changes, let's consider first the original meaning of the
verse and its context.

At Mount Sinai, God showed Moses the heavenly tabernacle and
instructed him to build a similar structure on earth. God warned
Moses to carefully follow the pattern shown to him on the mountain
(Exodus 25:9,40; Acts 7:44; Hebrews 8:5). The structure was to be a rec-
tangular tent with a single entryway and no windows. Inside, a curtain
was to divide the structure into a large outer room and a smaller inner
room. This earthly tabernacle was to serve as the focal point of Israel's
worship (Exodus 25:8; 29:42). Each day Jewish priests were to enter its
outer room and perform various duties (Exodus 30:7-8; Leviticus 4:18;
24:1-9). Once a year on the Day of Atonement, the Jewish high priest
was to enter the inner room and present the blood of sin offerings
to make atonement for himself and for the Jewish nation (Leviticus
16:1-34). In front of the tabernacle, God told Moses to construct a
bronze altar upon which the priests were to continually offer animal
sacrifices (Numbers 28–29).

Hebrews 9 reviews these details. The emphasis in this chapter is on
the *frequency* with which the Jewish priests were required to enter the
tabernacle and perform these duties. There we read, "Now when these
things have been so prepared, the priests are *continually entering* the
outer tabernacle performing the divine worship, but into the second,
only the high priest enters *once a year,* not without taking blood, which
he offers for himself and for the sins of the people committed in
ignorance" (Hebrews 9:6-7, emphasis added). The verses that follow

contrast this continual and yearly ministry of the Jewish priests in the earthly tabernacle with the once-for-all ministry of the Lord Jesus in the heavenly tabernacle. The writer of Hebrews concludes:

> But when Christ appeared as a high priest of the good things to come, He entered through the greater and more perfect tabernacle, not made with hands, that is to say, not of this creation; and not through the blood of goats and calves, but through His own blood, He *entered* the holy place *once for all, having obtained* eternal redemption (Hebrews 9:11-12, emphasis added).

These verses speak of an event that immediately followed Christ's crucifixion. The Lord Jesus entered into the presence of God in the heavenly tabernacle. There He presented His shed blood on our behalf (Hebrews 9:24-25). Unlike the Jewish priests, however, who "are continually entering" (Hebrews 9:6) the earthly tabernacle, and unlike the high priest, who "enters once a year" (Hebrews 9:7), the Lord Jesus, our High Priest, entered the heavenly tabernacle "once for all, having obtained eternal redemption" (Hebrews 9:12). Only one presentation of His blood was necessary, for God the Father accepted it as the perfect and complete payment for our sins.

Now consider how Pope John Paul II altered the meaning of Hebrews 9:12. He wrote that "Jesus Christ constantly 'enters into God's sanctuary thus obtaining eternal redemption'" (cf. Hebrews 9:12)."[40] As stated before, three significant changes are apparent.

First, the pope introduces the quote with the word *constantly,* writing that "Jesus Christ constantly 'enters into God's sanctuary'" (cf. Hebrews 9:12)."[41] He then omits the words "once for all," lest they clash with his "constantly." The verse says Christ "entered the holy place once for all" (Hebrews 9:12). In Hebrews 9 it is the Jewish priests who are *constantly* entering the tabernacle. This is contrasted by the Holy Spirit in Hebrews 9 with the Lord Jesus, who entered once. Nonetheless, the pope has Christ entering "constantly."

Second, the former pope said Christ "enters" God's sanctuary, using the present tense. The original text of Hebrews 9:12 says that Christ "entered" God's sanctuary, using the past tense. In the original Greek text, the verb is in the aorist tense, which portrays Christ's entrance into the heavenly sanctuary as an event in past time, freezing the action as if it took place within a snapshot of time. The pope, however, not finding this to his liking, simply changed the tense of the verb to the present, writing that Christ "enters into God's sanctuary." This makes Christ's entrance an event now occurring, an action now in progress.

Third, John Paul changed the ending of the verse to teach that by constantly entering the heavenly sanctuary, Jesus Christ is "thus obtaining eternal redemption." Once again Christ's work of redemption is pictured as a work in progress. Christ is "obtaining" it. The Bible, however, teaches the opposite. It says Christ entered the holy place once for all, "having obtained eternal redemption." It presents the work of redemption as an accomplished feat. It's done!

Now why would the pope change the Scriptures? Why would he want Catholics to think the Bible teaches Christ "constantly 'enters into God's sanctuary thus obtaining eternal redemption'" instead of what it actually teaches, that Christ "entered the holy place once for all, having obtained eternal redemption"? Because Rome holds that salvation is an ongoing process. The Church must *constantly* represent Christ as a victim in the Sacrifice of the Mass for our salvation. With each offering, some 120 million times a year, the Church says that "the work of our redemption is continually carried out."[42] So the pope, not finding Hebrews 9:12 to his liking, simply changed it! This was not a slip of the pen, but a calculated alteration of God's Word to suit his purposes and to make the Mass appear biblical. With such teaching from the supposed vicar of Christ and infallible teacher of the Church, is it any wonder that Catholics such as Anthony can't see any contradictions between what the Church says and what the Bible says?

The Water and Wine of the Chalice

Consider yet another unbiblical practice of the Roman Catholic Mass. During the central part of the Mass, the Liturgy of the Eucharist, the altar server pours wine and a little water into the chalice. The priest then says quietly over the chalice, "By the mystery of this water and wine may we come to share in the divinity of Christ, who humbled himself to share in our humanity." He then elevates the chalice slightly over the altar, and says, "Blessed are you, Lord, God of all creation. Through your goodness we have this wine to offer, fruit of the vine and work of human hands. It will become our spiritual drink." We have already considered the blood and the sacrificial character of the Mass, but why the water? What's that about?

During the sixteenth century, the Catholic Church convened the Council of Trent to counter the criticism of Luther, Calvin, and the other Reformers. Among the topics the Council addressed was the practice of adding water to the wine of the chalice. You can read the Council's defense of this practice in the official documents of the Council of Trent. They are readily available on the Internet. One of the best sites for Catholic documents is the website of the Eternal Word Television Network (www.ewtn.com). Check under "Libraries." You can find the Church's defense for adding water to the wine in the record of the Documents of the Council of Trent, Session 22, "The Doctrine Concerning the Sacrifice of the Mass," chapter 7. The document states that the priest is to mix water with the wine for three reasons.

The first is because the Church believes that Christ did this at the Last Supper. He placed water into the cup which He blessed, and then passed it on to His disciples. The document does not provide scriptural support for this belief, for there is none.

The second reason for adding water, according to the Church, is because when the Roman soldier pierced Christ's side with a spear, blood and water came forth. The Church cites John 19:34 in support of this.

The third reason is unexpected and scandalous. The official document states: "The holy council in the next place calls to mind that the Church has instructed priests to mix water with the wine that is to be offered in the chalice...since in the Apocalypse of St. John the 'people' are called 'waters,' the union of the faithful people with Christ their head is [thereby] represented."

The reference here to the Apocalypse of St. John is a reference to the book of Revelation. A footnote in the document refers the reader to Revelation 17:1 and 17:15. The context of that chapter is the end times and the reign of the Antichrist. Aligned with him is a false religious system referred to figuratively in Revelation 17 as a woman with the name "Babylon the Great, the Mother of Harlots" (Revelation 17:5). The first verse referred to by the Council of Trent with regard to the "waters" states, "Come here, I will show you the judgment of the great harlot who sits on many waters" (Revelation 17:1). The second reads, "The waters which you saw where the harlot sits, are peoples and multitudes and nations and tongues" (Revelation 17:15). And so the "waters" do indeed represent people, but they are the people subject to the great harlot! It is these that the Council equates with "the faithful people," that is, the Roman Catholic people. One can only wonder what the learned bishops of the Council were thinking when they offered this reason for adding water to the wine.

Further, since according to Catholic doctrine the wine within the chalice becomes Christ's blood and is offered to God the Father in sacrifice, mingling water with it that represents the Catholic people results in an offering that is a mixture of Christ and sinful men. This is what is offered to God. As strange as it might sound, such an offering is consistent with Catholic theology, which teaches that all human suffering is redemptive. Pope John Paul II wrote,

> Every man has his own share in the Redemption...In
> bringing about the Redemption through suffering,

Christ has also raised human suffering to the level of the Redemption. Thus each man, in his suffering, can also become a sharer in the redemptive suffering of Christ (*Salvifici Doloris*, no. 19).

How Will They Know?

Who's going to tell people like Anthony the truth? Who's going to talk to them about the finished work of Christ and salvation in His perfect and unique offering for sin? Scripture tells us that it is the responsibility of those who know Christ to tell others of Him. Christ has commissioned us as His ambassadors, saying, "All authority has been given to Me in heaven and on earth. Go therefore and make disciples of all the nations, baptizing them in the name of the Father and the Son and the Holy Spirit, teaching them to observe all that I commanded you; and lo, I am with you always, even to the end of the age" (Matthew 28:18-20). This is an awesome task. The Lord Himself, however, accompanies us in enabling us to effectively represent Him. "The weapons of our warfare," the Scriptures state, "are not of the flesh, but divinely powerful for the destruction of fortresses" (2 Corinthians 10:4). Those weapons are the Word of God and prayer. When wielded in the power of the Holy Spirit, they are indeed powerful.

I've lost track of Anthony, but not his sister Teresa, who continues to walk with the Lord. I phoned her today to get an update. In recent years, three of her sisters have come to Christ. Anthony, she told me, has left the Catholic Church. He now attends a church where the Bible is taught and Christ is exalted as risen, a Savior who has completed the only necessary sacrifice for sin.

9

We Got It in a Flash!

The lights came on for Bernard Bush one evening at Mass. A retired pharmacist some 80 years of age, he and his wife, Ann, faithfully attended each week. They supported the Church with their finances and volunteered in the parish when needed. They raised their three sons in the Catholic faith, two of whom entered the Catholic priesthood. Bernard and Ann—both intelligent, well-taught, confident, and outspoken—were proud of their sons and their Church.

They were also in great spiritual darkness—the deep darkness of false religion. They knelt before idols and repeated mantra-like prayers; offered weekly sacrifices to atone for the sins of the living and the dead; venerated bones, teeth, and locks of hair; spent hours in silent adoration of inanimate objects such as bread; prayed to the dead; and carried fetishes to ward off evil and secure favors from on high. And although they were aware that such practices are found in the occult, it never occurred to them that what they were doing might be just as wrong, for they, like Anthony in the previous chapter, did all these things within the context of the Roman Catholic Church.

The Lord brought the light of the gospel into Bernard and Ann's lives through their son Bob, a Jesuit of some 30 years. He had entered the religious order, formally known as the Society of Jesus, right out of high school. His hope was to find a meaningful relationship with God and peace within. Thirty years later he was still looking. Despite the best training the Catholic Church had to offer, including doctoral work in Rome and ordination into the Catholic priesthood, Bob knew in his heart that something was missing. In 1970 he became involved in the Catholic charismatic renewal. It was just getting underway, and the excitement of the new movement drew Bob in. Soon he was leading a group of over 1000 people, who met in the gymnasium of the high school where he taught.

"When it began," Bob now recounts, "people were hungry for God. The focus was on praying directly to God and the reading of Scripture. Many were touched by God and the power of His Word." Bob was so enthusiastic about what he was learning from the Word that he told his parents about it. Soon they also were reading the Bible.

At first Bernard and Ann found Bible reading slow going. Unfamiliar with the stories and the style, they found it difficult. But in time the living Word of God captivated their minds and hearts. Ann wore the cover off her Bible, reading it from one end to the other repeatedly. Often she would stop and say to Bernard, "Listen to how beautiful this is." She would then read him a few verses of Scripture. He began doing the same for her.

One evening several years later, Bob asked to speak with his parents. He had been a Jesuit 34 years by then. "Mom, Dad, as you know, I've been doing a lot of studying lately," Bob began, "and a lot of thinking. Recently I made a decision I want you to know about. I've decided to leave the priesthood and the Catholic Church." It was a moment Bob had dreaded for weeks, not wanting to hurt his elderly parents or disappoint them. But God had made it clear to Bob that he could no longer continue as a Catholic.

"Well, Bob," Bernard said slowly, "you know your mother and I have also been reading the Bible. We're not as far along as you, but we support you in your decision." They exchanged cautious smiles, aware that God was doing something special in their lives.

The following Saturday evening, Bernard and Ann went to Mass as they usually did, but that night there was nothing usual about it. The parish was about to begin a novena (nine days of special prayers and devotions) to Saint Anne, the woman the Church says was the mother of Mary. Before Mass began, in preparation for the novena, the parish priest led a solemn procession to the front of the church, escorting a visiting statue of Saint Anne. Bernard immediately began to feel uneasy.

We don't even know who Mary's mother was, he thought to himself, *so why are we having a novena to her?* He watched as parishioners placed the statue on a pedestal at the front of the church. Then, laying bouquets of flowers at the statue's feet, they knelt before it, offering prayers and veneration to Saint Anne. Suddenly, as if someone had turned on the lights, everything in the church took on a different meaning for Bernard.

What are we doing with that statue in the church? Bernard asked himself. *And those people up there, what they're doing is pure idolatry. It's wrong. God forbids it. In fact, what are we doing with statues in here at all? What's happened to us? And what's that altar doing in here? We're not supposed to have an altar. Sacrifice went out with the dying of Christ on the cross. And who does that man up there think he is, all dressed up in vestments like the pagan priests of Rome?*

One familiar sight after another struck Bernard in a new light. Things he had never questioned now seemed patently wrong. He turned to his wife. "Let's get out of here," he said. "We don't belong. I don't know why I never realized it before."

From Darkness into Light

For some 80 years, Bernard accepted the Catholic Church as the representative of God on earth. He never questioned any of the aforementioned practices. But now, having read God's Word for himself, it all came together. Bernard later said of that night:

> We were blessed, both my wife and I, by a gift of the Holy Spirit. We had no right to have it and couldn't have earned it. Unlike many, we didn't have to go through all of the stages of doubting and all the struggles that people normally go through. We just got it in a flash! Both my wife and I got the same gift at the same moment. We saw the errors of Catholicism. We saw the whole situation from Jesus' eyes, rather than our eyes.

Bernard and Ann's son, Bob, had a similar experience. "I prayed and prayed," Bob recalls, "asking God to help me see clearly what I should do, what was right and what was wrong."

God answered that prayer. Bob now believes that no Catholic can understand the truth unless God first opens his eyes. He puts it this way:

> Catholics need a revelation. They are so convinced that what they're doing is right they need God to help them see the truth. It's like Matthew 16, where Peter confessed that Jesus was the Christ. Jesus told Peter, "Blessed are you, Simon Barjona, because flesh and blood did not reveal this to you, but My Father who is in heaven." Jesus is explaining for us and for people of all time that going to school, studying theology, doing good works, feeding the poor, giving away all your money—it doesn't matter what you do—none of these things can open a person's mind to see the truth. It comes from God.

How Great Is the Darkness?

Though the Scriptures are read at Mass and Bible studies are sometimes offered through the parish, most Catholics don't even have a passing knowledge of the Bible. Few ever read the whole book. Most haven't even read the complete New Testament. That's the way it was for Bernard and Ann Bush. Bernard told me:

> As a child there never was a Bible in my house. I never saw a Bible. As an adult, I never had a Bible until I was almost 80. Now, you can't very well read something that isn't there. Things have changed somewhat, and I've found that today most Catholics do have a Bible. It's usually one of those beautiful Bibles that has all the decorations. It sits on the coffee table where everybody who comes into the house can see it. It has a record of births, confirmations, and deaths. Whenever I see one of those Bibles in a Catholic home, I ask, "When was the last time you opened it and read something?" "Oh, we don't open it," they tell me. "We don't read it." So they have the Bible there for looks. It's show. It's decoration. I haven't found one yet who reads it.

Such lack of biblical knowledge leaves Catholics open to spiritual deception. Without inspired Scripture to guide them, they are "carried about by every wind of doctrine" (Ephesians 4:14), unwittingly engaging in practices that have more in common with the occult than they do with biblical Christianity. The large number of Catholics who along with their Catholicism also practice spiritism, shamanism, voodoo, witchcraft, Santeria, and the like indicates that the problem is significant.

The Bible in Roman Catholicism

Some believe things are improving. Since the Second Vatican Council there has been a greater emphasis on the Bible in the Catholic Church. Parish Bible studies are now common. Children study the Bible in Catholic schools. For these things we can be thankful to God.

At the same time, however, it should be noted that Catholics are taught to approach the Bible in a different manner than evangelical Christians. The goal of Catholic Bible study is not to explore the Scriptures to discover what they teach, but rather to learn how the Scriptures present the teaching of the Church.

The focus of Catholic Bible studies can also vary widely. Jean and I first started attending our parish Bible study shortly after we married. We had been introduced to the study of the Scriptures through a home study sponsored by a small evangelical Bible church. Over a number of weeks we heard the gospel and came to saving faith in Christ. Excited about the truths of Scripture, we began attending our parish Bible study as well.

A few months later, disappointment began to set in. It turned out that our parish "Bible study" had more to do with planning wine and cheese parties and gambling trips to Reno than it did with Scripture study. Two years later, while the parish study was still wandering in circles, a new director of adult religious education was hired. He had a postgraduate degree in theology from Notre Dame. We were hopeful that finally we were going to move forward. The new leader announced that we would be studying the book of Job. A large group of parishioners showed up, eager to get started.

The first evening of the class, however, the new man made a startling confession. "I have to admit," he began, "I don't know why the book of Job is in the Bible. In my preparation for this course, I didn't get much out of it. But we're going to study it anyway, and see what happens."

Jean and I were stunned. How could anyone get nothing out of an inspired book? We were still attending the home Bible study through which we had come to know Christ. The teacher was a young man named Dale. Not much older than ourselves, he was a pipe fitter with the local utility company. We would meet at his home on Friday nights and discuss the Scriptures for an hour and a half. Each week we studied two or three verses from Ephesians. The time was filled with lively discussion and spiritual nourishment from God's Word. What a contrast to our learned Catholic teacher, who was now telling us that an entire book of the Bible was all but worthless. The comparison was striking. We decided that night that we had had enough of Catholic Bible study. We left the Church a short time later.

Parish studies can actually be detrimental to seeking Catholics. Often the reason they are started is to counteract evangelical studies in the neighborhood. The priest, having learned that parishioners are studying the Bible with non-Catholics, decides to regather his flock by starting a study of his own in the church hall. It is not unusual for the teacher at such studies to begin by undermining the authority and credibility of the Scriptures in an effort to bring lost sheep back under the authority of Rome. I have seen priests mock "Bible Christians" and "fundamentalists" who take everything in the Scriptures so literally they can't tell the difference between plain and figurative language. At one Catholic study I visited, the priest raised a Bible and announced, "The Catholic Church is not a Bible-based church." His words were directed at Steve and Patty, parish youth leaders who had invited me to the study. They had been reading the Bible and bringing their questions to the priest. Apparently they had challenged the Church's authority one too many times. The priest wanted them and everyone else in attendance to know he wasn't going to tolerate anyone judging the Church by the Bible. He then proceeded to explain how the Bible is a difficult book, full of myths and errors. It was questionable, he said, if even the words of Jesus in the Gospels were authentic. Wise Catholics, he advised, leave Bible interpretation to the Church's scholarly bishops.

The purpose of such denigration of the Bible and Bible-believing Christians is to inoculate seeking Catholics against evangelization. The tactic is effective. Those using it, however, will one day have to give an account to the Lord, who pronounced judgment upon the Pharisees for doing the same, saying, "You shut off the kingdom of heaven from people; for you do not enter in yourselves, nor do you allow those who are entering to go in" (Matthew 23:13).

Catholic Charismatic Renewal

Some good did come out of the Catholic charismatic renewal. The large numbers of born-again former charismatic Catholics now in evangelical churches attest to this. In the early days of the renewal, the late sixties and early seventies, it was largely a lay movement. Many Catholics began to seek God and read the Scriptures. The renewal spread quickly throughout the world.

All that changed in the late seventies as bishops issued directives to bring the movement firmly under Church control. They assigned liaisons to each parish group to keep watch and guard Catholic orthodoxy. Teaching from Church-authorized books replaced the Scriptures. Clergy became more visible in the leadership. Spontaneous praying was out, the rosary was in. Devotion to Mary and the celebration of the Mass became the focus.

"What happened," Bob Bush recounts, "was that everything got watered down and compromised. There was no longer any power in the movement. People stopped hearing from the Holy Spirit. They weren't having the radical changes in their lives as before. The renewal became just another form of Catholicism."

A more traditional priest was assigned to lead Bob's prayer group. Within a short time, the group went from over 1000 to just a few handfuls of people. Bob left the Catholic Church a short time later.

How You Can Help

1. Knowing which Bible passages will be read at Mass each
Sunday can be a useful aid when talking to Catholics. The
Church determines the readings. This means that on a
given day the readings are the same in every Catholic
Church throughout the world. The readings are on a three-
year cycle, known as Years A, B, and C. The rotation is sometimes printed at the back of Catholic Bibles. You can also
find it on the Internet, at sites such as the one for the
Catholic New American Bible (www.nccbuscc.org/nab).

Each Sunday there are three readings. The first is usually
from the Old Testament, the second from the New
Testament epistles, and the third from one of the four
Gospels. Take special note of the Gospel reading, as it
receives the most emphasis at Mass and is often the topic
of the priest's homily or sermon.

You can use this information when talking to Catholics.
Here are some questions you might ask:

- What was the Gospel reading at Mass on Sunday
about?

- I noticed that the Gospel reading at Mass last Sunday
included Mark 10:45, one of my favorite verses. There
Christ says that He came to give "His life a ransom for
many." Did the priest happen to mention that in his
homily?

- I've been following the readings at Mass. I noticed
that one of my favorite sections will be read next
Sunday, John 3:16-18. Let me know what you think of
it.

2. Catholics often admit they get little out of going to Mass. Others, having concluded that it is not worth the effort, stop going. Here are some questions you can ask your Catholic friends in order to better understand how they view the Mass and to help them think through its meaning.

   ◆ What does the Mass mean to you?

   ◆ Do you attend Mass weekly?

   ◆ What do you think happens to the bread and wine during the consecration?

   ◆ I understand that the Catholic Church teaches that the Mass is a real sacrifice, the sacrifice of Christ on the cross. Is that what you believe?

   ◆ As Christ died He cried, "It is finished!" (John 19:30). Why not celebrate that the work of redemption is finished, rather than trying to continue it in the Sacrifice of the Mass?

   And for the Catholic who no longer attends Mass regularly, you can ask:

   ◆ If the Mass is a form of worship which Christ instituted, why do you think so many people get so little out of it?

   ◆ Would you like to try a different form of Christian worship, something based more directly on Scripture?

3. Before speaking to your Catholic friend about God, speak to God about your Catholic friend. Jesus told two parables about prayer. Both emphasized the importance of being persistent (Luke 11:5-8; 18:1-8). Pray in faith, knowing that God hears you (1 Peter 3:12) and that "the effective prayer

of a righteous man can accomplish much" (James 5:16). Pray knowing that God "desires all men to be saved and to come to the knowledge of the truth" (1 Timothy 2:4). He is "not wishing for any to perish but for all to come to repentance" (2 Peter 3:9).

4. Use the opportunities God gives you to speak to your family and close friends about Christ, but don't overdo it. Though well intentioned, constant witnessing can do more harm than good, leaving Catholic family and friends thinking you are some kind of fanatic—a person "who can't change his mind and won't change the subject," as Churchill described the term. Seek the Spirit's guidance and pray for God-given opportunities to speak on His behalf. Pray that God would guide you. Then trust God for the outcome, knowing that effective evangelism is God working through you to His glory.

5. In witnessing to others, never forget that how you live your life is as important as what you say. When trying to reach family members, especially those in authority over you, keep Peter's instruction to women married to unsaved men in mind. He wrote, "You wives, be submissive to your own husbands so that even if any of them are disobedient to the word, they may be won without a word by the behavior of their wives, as they observe your chaste and respectful behavior" (1 Peter 3:1-2). In the same way that both wings of a plane are necessary for it to fly, so both your words and your life are important in effective evangelism.

Part Three

Talking to Catholics About Authority

10
Be Not Afraid

In 1993, Italian journalist Vittorio Messori was offered the opportunity of a lifetime. Pope John Paul II was about to celebrate the fifteenth anniversary of his papacy. To mark the occasion, an Italian television station invited the pope to participate in a special broadcast. It was to be the first time a journalist would interview the head of the Roman Catholic Church on live television. To the amazement of everyone involved, the pope accepted the invitation. Because of his extensive writings on Catholicism, Vittorio Messori was to have the privilege of conducting the interview.

In preparation for the event, Messori submitted a series of questions to Pope John Paul, outlining the course of the interview. A short time later the Vatican informed Messori that the pope had to withdraw. His many duties would not allow him to participate in the broadcast. But a few months later, Pope John Paul surprised those involved again, returning the interview questions to Messori with carefully written answers for each. The pope informed Messori, "I kept your questions on my desk. They interested me. I didn't think it would be wise to let them go to waste. So I thought about them and, after some time, during the brief moments when I was free from obligations, I responded to them in writing."[43] The pope suggested that the answers be released as a book and even suggested a title, *Crossing the Threshold of Hope*. A book agreement was drawn up and the answers were published in 1995. The book became an immediate international bestseller.

Crossing the Threshold of Hope opens with a remarkably frank question—one which Messori, aware that he was treading on sensitive ground, formed carefully:

> In front of me is a man dressed in the white of ancient custom, with a cross over his chest. This man who is called the *Pope* (from "father," in Greek) is a mystery in and of himself, a sign of contradiction. He is even considered a challenge or a "scandal" to logic or good sense by many of our contemporaries.[44]

Messori then described John Paul's position as pope, listing his many titles as "leader of the Catholic Church," "Vicar of Jesus Christ," "Holy Father," "Your Holiness," and "the man on earth who represents the Son of God, who 'takes the place' of the Second Person of the omnipotent God of the Trinity."[45] Messori continued, "Nevertheless, according to many others, this is an absurd and unbelievable claim.... You are either the mysterious living proof of the Creator of the universe or the central protagonist of a millennial illusion."[46]

Having set a provocative context, Messori then asked his first question, one which in earlier times would have been considered impertinent. "May I ask: Have you ever once hesitated in your belief in your relationship with Jesus Christ and therefore with God?"[47] Pope John Paul's answer was equally remarkable. He began, "Your question is infused with both a lively faith and a certain anxiety. I state right from the outset: 'Be not afraid!' "[48]

Those words—"Be not afraid!"—marked the papacy of John Paul II. He first proclaimed them publicly on October 22, 1978, in Saint Peter's Square as he began his reign as pope. He considered those three words, borrowed from the Gospels, an important theme of his papacy.

The pope continued in his answer to Messori's first question, saying,

> Have no fear when people call me the "Vicar of Christ," when they say to me "Holy Father," or "Your Holiness," or use titles similar to these, which seem even inimical to the Gospel. Christ himself declared: "Call no one on earth your father; you have but one Father in heaven. Do not be called 'Master'; you have but one master, the Messiah" (Matthew 23:9-10). These expressions, nevertheless, have evolved out of a long tradition, becoming part of common usage. One must not be afraid of these words either.[49]

Here John Paul acknowledges that his many titles and the exalted position that they represent may appear to be "inimical" or opposed to Scripture.[50] The pope even quotes in his answer Jesus' prohibition against the use of titles of religious superiority such as "teacher," "father," and "leader"—all used in Roman Catholicism of the pope. John Paul then dismisses any thought of impropriety with the words, "Be not afraid!" Like an all-wise father comforting an anxious child with a pat on the head, the pope assures the faithful that calling him "Holy Father" or "Your Holiness"—longstanding practices of the Church—is proper. Essentially he's telling the Catholic people, "Trust me! It's okay. I know. I'm the pope."

Others might still reasonably ask, How can the pope condone a practice that Jesus forbids? Furthermore, how can a "long tradition" justify disobedience to Scripture? Why are Catholics willing to accept such a weak explanation? The answers to each of these questions lie in the Roman Catholic understanding of revelation.

Revelation and the Church

Roman Catholicism teaches that Jesus Christ revealed the Christian faith in all its fullness to His 12 apostles. They in turn entrusted it to their successors, the bishops of the Roman Catholic Church. The pope, the bishop of Rome, together with the other bishops of the world, form a body known as the *magisterium*. Together they are the guardians, interpreters, and authoritative teachers of divine revelation.

The Church refers to the body of beliefs and practices entrusted to the pope and bishops as the "sacred deposit of faith." It says that the apostles passed down this deposit to the Catholic people and their bishops in two distinct ways. The first was through *unwritten* means, such as the apostles' preaching, conduct, prayer, and worship. The Church refers to that portion of revelation received from Christ and passed on by the apostles through unwritten means as Tradition. The second form in which the apostles passed down the revelation received from Christ was in *written* forms. The Holy Spirit moved men to record a portion of the deposit of faith as the inspired writings of the New Testament. The Church teaches that Scripture and Tradition together form the *Word of God*. Together they preserve the entire sacred deposit of faith and serve the Church "as the supreme rule of her faith."[51]

This explanation of revelation may sound reasonable to some, especially when Rome describes Tradition as nothing more than the apostles' preaching and example. The Church even cites Paul's teaching in support of its position: "So then, brethren, stand firm and hold to the traditions which you were taught, whether by word of mouth or by letter from us" (2 Thessalonians 2:15).

But look more closely at what the Roman Catholic Church means by Tradition, and you will find that it has little to do with what Paul means by "traditions" in 2 Thessalonians 2:15. There, Paul is writing to his contemporaries—to Christians living in Thessalonica whom he had personally taught. He tells them to hold fast to the "traditions" they received *from him*. The Greek word translated "traditions" simply means "something handed down." Paul uses the word to stress that the truths that he taught the Thessalonians did not originate with him. He simply passed on to them that which he had received from the Lord. This same explanation is true of two other verses often cited by the

Catholic Church to support its view of Tradition: 1 Corinthians 11:2 and 2 Thessalonians 3:6. These verses also speak of truths Paul received from the Lord and personally passed on to the first generation of Christians in Corinth and Thessalonica.

Is this what the Roman Catholic Church means by Tradition? Not at all. Catholic Tradition is not Paul's oral teachings, as if someone had been able to record his voice on some kind of first-century audio device. Neither is Catholic Tradition a firsthand account of the apostles' preaching, their conduct, or their worship. Then what is Roman Catholic Tradition? The question is not easily answered.

Roman Catholic Tradition Defined

The Church of Rome appears to be purposefully vague when describing Tradition. It is clear enough in its claim that the *source* of Tradition is the unwritten teachings of Christ and the apostles. But the source, as the Church knows well, is not the issue. *Transmission* is the issue. How has this alleged body of extrabiblical apostolic truths been passed down in unwritten forms for some 20 centuries? That's what we need to know. How can vital information be passed down for 2000 years in unwritten forms without being lost or corrupted? Where does this alleged unwritten sacred deposit of information currently reside? How can we get access to it? How can we check its authenticity and accuracy? These are the important questions concerning transmission.

As stated earlier, the answers to these questions are not easily found. Indeed, the Church is so evasive and vague when it comes to supplying answers that suspicion that all is not right is warranted. In brief, the Church answers them with one word—the Church! According to Catholic teaching, it is through the Church as a whole and the magisterium in particular that Tradition has been preserved, kept from corruption, and is made available to us today. The Church's understanding of revelation as a whole—Scripture and Tradition together—is so closely linked to the Church's understanding of itself that they cannot be separated. According to the Second Vatican

Council, "Sacred Tradition, sacred Scripture and the Magisterium of the Church are so connected and associated that one of them cannot stand without the others."[52]

In trying to grasp what the Church means by this, we must first understand what it means by Tradition. To begin with, don't think of Tradition as something you can pick up and read. Even today Tradition is *unwritten;* it is not contained in books, regardless how ancient they might be. Tradition may be *expressed* in the writings of the early Christians, such as the so-called "church fathers," but their writings are not Tradition itself. Remember, Tradition by its very nature is unwritten and will always be unwritten. The church fathers are simply "witnesses" to Tradition. The same is said of the early creeds, such as the Apostles' Creed. It may express what is contained in Tradition, but it is not Tradition itself. The same is true of ancient liturgies, inscriptions on monuments, and even the documents of various synods and the ecumenical councils. These express the doctrines and practices derived from Tradition, but they are not Tradition itself. Neither is Tradition the result of scholarly research performed by historians and archaeologists trying to reconstruct the beliefs and practices of the primitive church. Such may be said to be witnesses to Tradition and/or expressions of Tradition, but they are not in a formal sense Tradition itself.

So what is Tradition? Well, as we have seen, it's not exactly something you can lay your hands on. It's not even easily defined in words or conceptually grasped. Think of Tradition as something that resides within the Church, living at its very core. You might think of it as *the life experience of the Catholic people,* as some have described it. I realize this sounds rather vague, but don't give up yet. Understanding what the Church means by Tradition is essential to an understanding of Roman Catholicism.

Think of Tradition as the heartbeat of Roman Catholicism. It's what makes the whole thing tick. This is an image used by the Church to describe itself. The *Catechism of the Catholic Church* says Tradition is "written principally in the Church's heart rather than in documents and records."[53] Catholic theologians describe Tradition as "the word living continuously in the hearts of the faithful,"[54] a "current of life and truth coming from God through Christ and through the Apostles to the last of the faithful who repeats his creed and learns his catechism."[55] And so, to understand the Catholic concept of Tradition, you must think of it as something lived and experienced rather than something you can put down on paper and read.

Tradition lives within the Church, and for that reason only the "living magisterium" of the Church—the pope and bishops of Rome—can truly know it, define it, and explain it for the rest of us with infallible precision. Something similar can be said of Scripture, for again, only the magisterium of the Church has the authority and the ability to identify that which is genuinely Scripture, interpret it properly, and teach it with infallible authority. Accordingly, from a Catholic point of view, Tradition, Scripture, and the magisterium cannot be separated or even understood apart from one another.

Tradition and Scripture Together

This unwritten lived experience, what the Church calls Tradition, is what the Vatican would have us place alongside the written texts of the Bible. Never mind that such a concept is totally foreign to the Scriptures. Never mind that Jesus identified Scripture as the Word of God (John 10:35), but never Tradition. Disregard the fact that Jesus condemned the Jews with scathing criticism for elevating their Tradition to the same level of authority as God's written Word (Mark 7:1-13). Disregard the fact that the Church's understanding of Tradition is so vague and ethereal that the average Catholic hasn't a clue what the bishops mean by it. Never mind, for according to Rome's bishops, "both Scripture and Tradition must be accepted and honored with equal feelings of devotion and reverence."[56]

The Church is unmoved by accusations that its concept of

Tradition cannot be found in the Bible. It reminds its opponents that in Roman Catholicism not all beliefs need be explicitly taught in Scripture. In the words of the Second Vatican Council, "the Church does not draw her certainty about all revealed truths from the holy Scriptures alone."[57] Catholicism, says the *Catechism of the Catholic Church* is not a "religion of the book."[58] Commenting on this portion of the *Catechism,* Pope Benedict, then-Cardinal Joseph Ratzinger, wrote, "This is an extremely important affirmation. The faith does not refer simply to a book, which as such would be the sole and final appeal for the believer.[59]

In Roman Catholicism, beliefs and practices can be established from Tradition. They need not be plainly taught in Scripture. This means, of course, that Rome's doctrine of Tradition itself need not be explicitly found in the Bible. It can be infallibly defined (that is, without the possibility of error) by the magisterium based on revelation passed down in unwritten forms—you guessed it!—based on Tradition.

Such self-validation, of course, is meaningless. It is circular reasoning, using Tradition to prove the authority of Tradition. Only someone with absolute faith in the magisterium would be willing to accept such an argument. Such a person, however, would first have to be willing to accept the magisterium's own claims to ultimate and infallible teaching authority. Since these claims cannot be established from Scripture, however, the Church must turn again to Tradition to prove them. And so the cycle repeats in another meaningless loop—*Tradition is the Word of God. We know this for the magisterium teaches it, and the magisterium is God's authoritative and infallible teacher. We know this for Tradition teaches it, and Tradition is the Word of God.*[60]

The Church's Wild Card

Whenever it can, the Catholic Church uses Scripture to prove its doctrines. When it can't, it uses Tradition. Tradition is the Church's ace in the hole. When played, it trumps all arguments. It's an exceptionally versatile card, for Tradition is whatever the Church says it is. No one can say otherwise. In that sense it's like a joker, that wild card in the deck which, when needed, you can designate to be whatever you want it to be. It can establish the bishop of Rome as the vicar of Christ with jurisdiction over Christians everywhere. It can establish the teaching authority of the magisterium. When needed, Tradition can prove that there is a place called purgatory, where people can atone for their sins after death. It can establish the necessity of seven sacraments, each instituted by Christ and channels of grace necessary for salvation. Tradition can prove the sacrificial nature of the Mass and the miraculous change of bread and wine into the "real presence." The Church has used it to define as dogma (a binding doctrine that all Catholics must believe) the immaculate conception of Mary (defined in 1854), papal infallibility (defined in 1870), and the assumption of Mary into heaven (defined in 1950). What's next? Who knows!

Some say the Church may define as dogma the Catholic teaching that Mary is the co-redeemer of the human race. Should that be the case, no one will be able to say otherwise, for the Church will establish it from Tradition. Opposing arguments from Scripture will mean nothing, for the interpretation of Scripture, says the Church, "is ultimately subject to the judgment of the Church."[61] The Bible, says Rome, must be read within "the living Tradition of the whole Church."[62] Tradition is the key to interpreting the Bible, and should anyone challenge a belief or practice such as addressing a mere man as "Holy Father," the man dressed in white and holding that key will assure him that all is right, saying, "Be not afraid!"

11

Lord, I Apologize in Advance

Though thousands of people leave the Roman Catholic Church each year, some join it. Scott Hahn is one who joined. Raised in a Protestant family, an honor graduate of Gordon-Conwell Theological Seminary, and a Presbyterian minister, Hahn was an unlikely candidate to become a Roman Catholic. Nonetheless, at a 1986 Easter vigil held at Saint Bernard's Catholic Church in Milwaukee, Wisconsin, Hahn received what he describes as a "sacramental grand slam":[63] baptism, confession, confirmation, and Holy Communion. According to Catholic theology, that was the day he became a Roman Catholic. I think it was somewhat earlier.

Scott Hahn's journey into the Church of Rome began during his seminary years. Despite his Protestant upbringing, Hahn's studies led him to reject the belief that sinners could find acceptance before God simply by trusting Jesus. He concluded that a person comes into a right relationship with God by faith *and* works. Salvation, as Hahn came to understand it, was a covenant with God in which Christ shared His divine sonship with a new family. This compared well, Hahn thought, with Catholic teaching.

Already an admirer of the Vatican's stand against artificial birth control, Hahn decided to investigate Roman Catholicism further. He studied the Catholic doctrine of the real presence of Christ in the Eucharist, the ongoing Sacrifice of the Mass, and the papacy. After long months of comparing these and other Catholic doctrines to Scripture, Hahn concluded that Rome was right on every one of them. He recalls, "I had worked literally through, I would guess, a hundred different doctrines that the Catholic Church taught, that the Protestant Church rejected, and I came out Catholic on every one of them. In spite of them being Catholic, I just felt that they were faithful to Scripture."[64]

Hahn began thinking about converting to Roman Catholicism, but first he had to resolve a few more issues. The most fundamental one was the question of authority: Who or what determines how the faith received from Christ is to be understood and practiced?

For much of his early life Hahn had held that the Bible, as illuminated by the Holy Spirit, was the Christian's standard of truth and source of all teaching necessary for salvation and life. Now the Roman Catholic Church was confronting Hahn with a different answer. It said the faith received from Christ was to be found in Scripture *plus* Tradition—the sacred Tradition of the Roman Catholic Church. As interpreted by the popes and bishops of Roman Catholicism, Scripture and Tradition together were the supreme rule or standard of religious truth.

Who was right? Hahn settled the matter when he decided on another distinct doctrine of Roman Catholicism—devotion to Mary. Of all the Catholic doctrines he had investigated, he was finding those about Mary the most difficult to accept. Hahn writes, "Catholics have no idea how hard Marian doctrines and devotions are for Bible Christians."[65] He has said the role of Mary in Catholicism, as understood by Protestants, is "by far the most incomprehensible, offensive, and patently unbiblical superstition going."[66]

Mary, Mary, Quite Contrary

Hahn's point is well-taken. Christians familiar with the Bible find little resemblance between the Mary of Scripture and the Mary of Roman Catholicism. The real Mary was a faithful servant of God who humbly yielded herself as "the bondslave of the Lord" (Luke 1:38). Rome's Mary possesses godlike attributes and abilities. Her power, according to Pope Leo XIII, is "all but unlimited."[67] Pope John Paul II wrote that "Christ will conquer through her, because He wants the Church's victories now and in the future to be linked to her."[68] According to Pope Pius IX, Mary is

immaculate in every respect; innocent, and verily most innocent; spotless, and entirely spotless; holy and removed from every stain of sin; all pure, all stainless, the very model of purity and innocence; more beautiful than beauty, more lovely than loveliness; more holy than holiness, singularly holy and most pure in soul and body; the one who surpasses all integrity and virginity; the only one who has become the dwelling place of all the grace of the most Holy Spirit. God alone excepted, Mary is more excellent than all, and by nature fair and beautiful, and more holy than the Cherubim and Seraphim. To praise her all the tongues of heaven and earth do not suffice.[69]

Alleged supernatural appearances of Mary, known among Catholics as *apparitions*, have spurred devotion to her. These include Lourdes, France (1858); Fatima, Portugal (1917); and Medjugorje, Bosnia-Herzegovina (since 1981). In 1854, Pope Pius IX formally proclaimed the doctrine of Mary's *Immaculate Conception* as dogma, saying God had preserved Mary from all stain of inherited sin from Adam from the first instant of her conception. As a result, she lived a sinless life. Then in 1950, Pope Pius XII defined the doctrine of Mary's *assumption* as dogma, saying that at the end of her earthly life she was taken bodily into heaven.

The Catholic Church also honors Mary as "ever" virgin. Not only did she remain a virgin "until she gave birth" (Matthew 1:25), but afterward, though married to Joseph. The Church teaches that Jesus' birth was as miraculous as His conception. Mary experienced no pain and maintained her "virginal integrity inviolate."[70] The Church says the infant passed through her as sunrays pass through glass. One would think there was something scandalous about normal childbirth.

The Church further exalts Mary as the Mother of God, Mother of the Church, and even co-Redeemer of Mankind, explaining:

> Mary suffered and, as it were, nearly died with her suffering Son; for the salvation of mankind she renounced her mother's rights and, as far as it depended on her, offered her Son to placate divine justice; so we may well say that she with Christ redeemed mankind.[71]

Presently, says the Church, Mary sits crowned in heaven as the Queen of Heaven and Earth. There she serves as "the most powerful mediatrix and advocate of the whole world with her Divine Son."[72] She is the Mother of Grace through whom Christ grants all graces to the world. The Church says that Catholics should entrust all their cares and petitions to Mary, surrendering the hour of their death "wholly to her care."[73]

At the funeral Mass of Pope John Paul II, Cardinal Joseph Ratzinger, the soon-to-be Pope Benedict XVI, ended his homily by praying to the deceased pope, "We entrust your dear soul to the Mother of God, your Mother, who guided you each day and who will guide you now to the eternal glory of her Son, our Lord Jesus Christ. Amen."[74] The prayer was fitting, for Pope John Paul II chose as the Latin motto of his papacy *Totus Tuss,* meaning, with reference to Mary, "Totally yours." It was an expression of his complete consecration to the Blessed Virgin. Likewise, Pope Benedict began his reign by praying, "I invoke the maternal intercession of Mary most holy, in whose hands I place the present and the future of my person and of the church."[75]

Experimental Prayer

How did Scott Hahn come to embrace the Mary of Roman Catholicism? Late one night alone in his office, Hahn was pondering the Catholic doctrines about Mary. Throughout his life he had used the Scriptures as his guide. That night, however, unable to find agreement between Roman Catholic teaching and the Bible on the topic of Mary, he decided to try a new approach to knowing truth. He writes, "So many doctrines of the Catholic Church had proven to be sound biblically that I decided to step out in faith on this one."[76]

Hahn locked the door to his office and, in preparation for what he was about to do, prayed, "Lord, the Catholic Church has gotten it right 99 times out of a hundred. The only major obstacle left is Mary. I don't see it on this point. But I am going to give them the benefit of the doubt. I'm going to cut them some slack, and I'm going to say a prayer."[77]

Hahn then spoke to Mary, informing her of his intentions, saying, "Mary, if you're up there and this is wrong, don't be offended."[78] Once more Hahn spoke to God, fearful that he might be making a big mistake: "Most of all, God, if this upsets You, please, I'm sincere. Lord, I apologize in advance if You're offended by what I'm about to do."[79]

What Scott Hahn was about to do was to pray to someone other than God. He was going to ask Mary to resolve a private personal problem he was dealing with at the time. He prayed: "Mary, if you are even half of what the Catholic Church says, please take this specific petition—which seems impossible—to the Lord for me through this prayer."[80] Then, with a plastic set of beads in his hand and a booklet as his guide, he began to say the rosary, a collection of Catholic prayers, the primary one being the "Hail Mary." Hahn prayed: "Hail Mary, full of grace, the Lord is with thee. Blessed art thou among women and blessed is the fruit of thy womb, Jesus. Holy Mary, Mother of God, pray for us sinners now and at the hour of our death. Amen." While praying the rosary that night, he repeated "Hail Mary" 53 times, the "Our Father" six times, and a prayer called the "Glory Be" six times. In the days that followed, Scott Hahn prayed the rosary several more times, each time asking Mary to intercede for him. The result, he writes, was astounding: "Three months later, I realized that from the day I prayed my first rosary, that seemingly impossible situation had been completely reversed. My petition had been granted!" Hahn has prayed the rosary every day since, commenting, "It is a most powerful prayer—an incredible weapon."

That first rosary for Scott Hahn was more than his first prayer to someone other than God. For with that rosary, Hahn crossed over the threshold into the Roman Catholic Church—not because of the prayer itself, but because of what it signified. Consider the events leading to his decision to pray the rosary to Mary.

As Hahn locked the door to his office, his conscience was already bothering him. This is evident from the fact that he asked God to forgive him for what he was about to do. He knew the Bible didn't teach the Catholic doctrines about Mary and that there wasn't a single example in the Scriptures of anyone praying to her or anyone else other than God. He decided to do it anyway. *He did it because the Roman Catholic Church said it was the right thing to do.* He decided to trust Rome rather than God's written Word. In his own words: "So many doctrines of the Catholic Church had proven to be sound biblically that I decided to step out in faith on this one."[81] This was an act of submission and of faith in the Roman Catholic Church.

That decision represented a radical change in Hahn's methodology for knowing spiritual truth. Despite what he himself believed the Scriptures said was true, Hahn decided to trust what the Church of Rome said was true. No longer would he look first and foremost to the Bible. Now Scripture and Tradition together, as interpreted by the magisterium (the pope and bishops), would be his guide to truth. As to future Bible study, he would use the Church's supreme rule for interpretation: The authentic meaning of any verse of Scripture is what the magisterium, the teaching office of the Church, says it means.

Scott Hahn's formal admission into the Roman Catholic Church a short time later resulted from his decision that night in his office. Since then he has become a crusader for Roman Catholicism. He has accepted a professorship at the Catholic Franciscan University of Steubenville, Ohio, has been introduced to the pope, has had his autobiography published by a Catholic publisher, and has traveled widely, conducting seminars on Catholicism. He may well become the best-known Catholic convert of his generation.

Understanding Roman Catholic Authority

The authority structure to which Scott Hahn submitted is a system founded upon the claim that God has appointed the bishops of the Roman Catholic Church as the successors of Christ's 12 apostles. The Church says that its bishops have inherited from the apostles three exclusive rights: *sanctifying power, ruling power,* and *teaching power.*

Sanctifying power, says the Church, gives the bishops the ability to make the faithful holy. This is primarily accomplished through the bishops' authority to ordain priests and to oversee the sacraments through which Catholics receive grace from God. The bishops sanctify the Church "by their prayer and work, by their ministry of the word and of the sacraments."[82]

Ruling power is the right of the bishops to govern and to shepherd. They do this individually over the particular churches assigned to them and collectively over the worldwide Church.

Teaching power enables the bishops to interpret revelation and to preach it with authority. They are the "heralds of faith"[83] and the "authentic teachers"[84] of the truths passed on by the apostles.

The bishops exercise these powers in communion with the pope and under his guidance. He is the visible head of the Catholic Church.

The pope is the high priest, the supreme ruler, and the primary teacher of the faith.

The pope has inherited his position, says the Church, from Saint Peter. Christ made Peter the head of the apostles when He said to him, "You are Peter, and upon this rock I will build My church" (Matthew 16:18). According to the Church, Peter later became the bishop of Rome and ruled the universal church. The present bishop of Rome is Peter's successor. He is called the *pope*, from the Greek word for *father*, because he is the father of all the faithful, including the other bishops.

The bishops, under the leadership of the pope, form the magisterium. This is the authoritative teaching body of the Church. The magisterium's mission is to safeguard the doctrines of the Church, to teach them to the people, and to keep the people from going astray. It claims the exclusive right to interpret God's Word and judge its authentic meaning. The Second Vatican Council stated:

> The task of giving an authentic interpretation of the Word of God, whether in its written form or in the form of Tradition, has been entrusted to the living teaching office of the Church alone. Its authority in this matter is exercised in the name of Jesus Christ.[85]

In order to fulfill this responsibility, the Church teaches that Christ has endowed its bishops with the gift of *infallibility*. This means that in matters of faith and morals, the bishops acting together are incapable of teaching error. The Church also considers the pope acting alone to be infallible. When speaking with regard to faith and morals in his official capacity as head of the Church, the pope does not err and cannot err.

Submission to Rome's claim to sanctifying, ruling, and teaching power is an essential part of what it means to be a Roman Catholic. This means, as it did for Scott Hahn, accepting what the Church says in matters of religious belief and morality, even if one's own understanding of Scripture is the very opposite. Consequently, the night

Scott Hahn prayed his first rosary, in essence he became a Roman Catholic. Everything else followed from that decision.

Catholic Authority and the Bible

Submission to Roman Catholic Authority Is Unbiblical

Despite the Church's confident assertions and Scott Hahn's well-publicized conversion, there is no biblical basis for the submission that Rome demands. Christ never instituted an authority structure such as the one Rome seeks to impose upon Catholics. The rock upon which Christ built His church was not Peter, but the Lord Himself. Though Peter was a leading figure among the apostles, he was never the head of the apostles. The Lord Jesus was their leader both while He was on earth and later after He ascended into heaven.

There is no biblical record of a college of bishops ruling the universal church under the leadership of a pope in Rome. Neither did the apostles ever ask anyone to submit to their teaching without question. They taught the first Christians to "examine everything carefully; hold fast to that which is good" (1 Thessalonians 5:21). John warned, "Beloved, do not believe every spirit, but test the spirits to see whether they are from God, because many false prophets have gone out into the world" (1 John 4:1). Paul also spoke against blind obedience, writing, "But even if we, or an angel from heaven, should preach to you a gospel contrary to what we have preached to you, he is to be accursed!" (Galatians 1:8).

The pope, on the other hand, expects Catholics to submit to him as Christ's representative. They are to receive the Church's teaching "with docility,"[86] treating the pope's dogmatic teaching as infallible, beyond even the possibility of error. Compare that with how Paul treated Peter, supposedly the first Roman Catholic pope. During a visit to the church in Antioch, Peter initially enjoyed warm fellowship with Gentile believers. But when legalistic Jewish Christians arrived from Jerusalem and refused to have close contact or to eat with Gentile

Christians, Peter became fearful and confused. He withdrew from the Gentiles and began to "hold himself aloof" (Galatians 2:12). The other Jewish Christians in the church of Antioch followed Peter's example and also broke off contact with the Gentile believers. When Paul saw what was happening, he realized that the very heart of what it meant to be a Christian was at stake. Paul opposed Peter "to his face" (Galatians 2:11), "in the presence of all" (verse 14). He accused Peter of "hypocrisy" (verse 13), of not being "straightforward about the truth of the gospel" (verse 14).

This incident demonstrates that the early church considered no one to be immune to error or beyond reprimand. Indeed, the Scriptures warn us that there are "false apostles, deceitful workers, disguising themselves as apostles of Christ" (2 Corinthians 11:13). In the book of Revelation, Christ commends the Ephesian Christians, saying, "You put to the test those who call themselves apostles, and they are not, and you found them to be false" (Revelation 2:2).

Submission to Roman Catholic Authority Is Illogical

Scott Hahn's decision to submit to Roman authority was not only unbiblical, it was illogical. Hahn describes how for months he compared Roman Catholic teaching to Scripture, concluding that "the Church has gotten it right 99 times out of a hundred."[87] In his judgment, "the Catholic Church had proven to be sound biblically."[88] Note the process Hahn used to reach his conclusion. *He studied the Bible and used it to judge the teachings of the Roman Catholic Church.* In so doing, he considered himself competent to interpret Scripture and apply that interpretation to the doctrines of the Catholic Church. He decided if they were right or wrong.

Put aside for a moment the conclusion he reached, and focus only on the method he used. *He treated Scripture alone as the standard of truth.* A Protestant minister at the time, he used a principle that has been known since the Reformation as *sola Scriptura,* meaning

"Scripture alone." He used the Bible as his supreme norm for establishing truth.

In becoming a Catholic, however, Hahn embraced a system that rejects *sola Scriptura*. Rome teaches that the Church alone is able to judge the true meaning of Scripture. It teaches that Scripture can be understood only in the light of Tradition. *No one can use the Bible to judge the Church*. Hahn has now adopted this position as his own. Today he is an outspoken critic of *sola Scriptura*.

In his renunciation of *sola Scriptura*, however, Hahn has renounced the very method that he used—or misused—in becoming a Catholic. Did he not use Scripture to judge the Church? Did he not say he found the Catholic Church right 99 times out of a hundred? Did he not use *sola Scriptura*, the method he then rejected and now criticizes?

Since Hahn now rejects *sola Scriptura*, one would think he would stop presenting himself as the diligent young seminary student who searched the Scriptures for his answers and found the truth. If he now believes that his method was faulty, one would think he would declare his conclusion also faulty, and retry the case using some better method. But herein lies the problem: What other method could he have used?

Who Judges the Judge?

If one cannot use the Scriptures as the standard by which to judge the claims of Rome, one must ask, How *is* a person to know whether the Roman Catholic Church is what it declares itself to be? The Church says, "The task of interpreting the Word of God authentically has been entrusted solely to the Magisterium of the Church, that is, to the Pope and to the bishops in communion with him."[89] If that's the case, what are the rest of us supposed to do? How are we to recognize the Roman Catholic Church as the one true church instituted by Christ? By what standard are the Church's many assertions to be judged? Are we to submit to Rome's authority simply because the Vatican *says* it is the one true Church?

Certainly not. With the Holy Spirit as our Teacher and the inspired Scriptures as our text, we can know the truth. We can follow the example of the early Bereans, who "received the word with great eagerness, examining the Scriptures daily to see whether these things were so" (Acts 17:11). This, of course, is the last thing that Rome wants people to do. It knows that when Catholics begin looking to the Bible for truth, comparing Roman Catholic doctrine to God's inspired Word, questions will arise.

For Mike Gendron, a devout Catholic actively involved in the Church, it started with an advertisement in a Dallas newspaper. Endowed with an analytical mind, in his university days Mike had pursued degrees in mathematics and business. But in the practice of his Catholic faith, he realized he had no reasons for what he believed. The newspaper advertisement told of a seminar to be conducted on the "Evidences for the Christian Faith." The instructor was Christian apologist Josh McDowell. Mike attended the seminar. It convinced him that the Bible was God's inerrant, inspired, authoritative Word. He returned home determined to confirm his Catholic faith through the study of Scripture.

It wasn't long, however, before Mike began to notice discrepancies between what the Bible said and what the Church said. When the differences became contradictions, Mike decided it was time to call his Uncle Charles, a Roman Catholic priest. Father Charles responded graciously to Mike's questions, explaining the Church's position. Mike was "pacified," as he now describes it. But as he continued to study the Scriptures, other issues arose. Again he called Father Charles, and again his uncle was able to put Mike's troubled mind to rest. This cycle repeated itself several times over the next three years. On one visit Uncle Charles made to Mike's home, Mike excitedly told him about his discovery in 1 Thessalonians 4:13-18 of the rapture—the coming of Christ for the church.

"What Bible are you reading?" Father Charles asked his nephew.

"The one you gave me for Christmas five years ago," Mike answered. "Here, look what it says."

Father Charles took a quick glance at the passage and dismissed it, saying, "God doesn't really mean what He says there." With that he got up and walked out of the room.

Mike decided that night the Bible, not the Church, would be his supreme guide to truth. He left the Roman Catholic Church and now runs an evangelistic ministry in Dallas called Proclaiming the Gospel.

Nadine, a woman who had served many years as a Eucharistic minister and head of the parents' committee for youth instruction, commonly referred to as the CCD (Confraternity of Christian Doctrine), had a similar experience. When God began drawing Nadine to Himself, she developed an insatiable appetite for Bible study. When she began seeing discrepancies between what the Church taught and what the Bible taught, a battle began to rage within her. Was she going to believe the Church or the Scriptures?

One day she came upon a card produced by the Catholic Church titled "Articles of Faith." It listed the major doctrines of Roman Catholicism. *I don't believe that,* she found herself thinking as she scanned the first item on the list. *The Bible doesn't teach that,* she decided about another. *This one isn't right either. Neither is that one. I can't believe these things,* she concluded. *They contradict the Scriptures. And if I can't accept the major doctrines of Roman Catholicism, how can I remain in the Catholic Church?*

After 50 years as a devout Catholic, Doctor Figueroa, a medical doctor in Guatemala, started reading the Bible. Determined to understand its message, he finished the entire Bible in just three weeks. "I was shocked to learn that salvation was of God," Doctor Figueroa told me. "It's by grace and not by anything that we do." He left the Catholic Church a short time later.

Though none of these Catholics—Mike, Nadine, and Dr. Figueroa —realized it at the time, each of them left the Roman Catholic Church the moment they put God's Word above the Catholic Church's teaching. Their later decision to leave the Church was the natural outcome, for they were no longer *Roman* Catholics.

Jesus Is the Rock

What did Jesus mean when He said to Peter, "You are Peter, and upon this rock I will build My church" (Matthew 16:18)? If one interprets this verse in isolation, it may seem that the Roman Catholic Church is right—that Christ said He would build His church on Peter. But when you read the verse in context, it becomes apparent that Jesus is teaching that He *Himself* is the rock upon which He will build His church. Consider the following:

- The context of Matthew 16:18 is not about Peter but Jesus and His identity as the Son of God. It begins with Jesus asking His disciples, "Who do people say that the Son of Man is?" (Matthew 16:13). They answer, "Some say John the Baptist; and others, Elijah; but still others, Jeremiah, or one of the prophets" (verse 14). Christ then asks them, "But who do you say that I am?" (verse 15). Peter answers, "You are the Christ, the Son of the living God" (verse 16). The passage concludes with Jesus warning His disciples "that they should tell no one that He was the Christ" (verse 20). It's all about Jesus.

- Jesus made a play on words when He said, "You are Peter [*petros*, a masculine noun meaning "boulder" or "detached stone"], and upon this rock [*petra*, a feminine noun meaning "bedrock" or "a mass of rock"] I will build My church" (Matthew 16:18). This change in words indicates that the rock on which Christ would build His church was someone far greater than Peter. The rock is Jesus.

- Every figurative use of the word *rock* in the Old Testament is a reference to deity. See, for example, Deuteronomy 32:4,15,18; 1 Samuel 2:2; 2 Samuel 22:32; Psalm 18:31; Isaiah 44:8. Jesus' Jewish apostles would have had that imagery in their minds as they interpreted His words.

- The New Testament makes several references to Jesus as a rock or the foundation of the church—see Romans 9:33; 1 Corinthians 3:11; 10:4; Ephesians 2:20; 1 Peter 2:6-8.

- There is no biblical record of Peter serving as the head of the apostles, the head of the Church, or ruling as the bishop of Rome.

12

Once a Catholic, Always a Catholic

Modern Catholics have become increasingly vocal in their displeasure with the Church's teaching on issues that affect their everyday lives, such as birth control and the ordination of women, neither of which are allowed by Rome. With respect to doctrines that they consider to be of a more theological nature, however, Catholics are generally content to let the Church teach what it deems right. Few are interested in the study of doctrine or could even explain terms such as *the sacred deposit of faith, Tradition,* and *the magisterium.* That's what I found when talking with Catholics outside Saint Joseph's Catholic Cathedral in San Jose, California. I asked them about the origin of their religious beliefs, the Bible, the pope, and the magisterium. The first question I asked was, "What is the source of Roman Catholic belief?"

Richard, a man of about 50, answered, "They come from the Scriptures. I'm sure there are theological interpretations in there, too," he said, "but I'd say primarily from Scripture."

Tony agreed. "The Bible. They're all in the Bible."

Pat, a middle-aged woman, shook her head when I asked whether she knew what was the source of Catholic teaching. "I wouldn't know how to answer that," she said.

Beatrice was just as much in the dark. "I really don't know. I suppose from Jesus' teaching. I don't know. To tell you the truth, I've never thought about that."

Mary Ann, a woman of about 40, was better informed about the origins of Catholic doctrine. "From Jesus Christ and His apostles," she told me. "We know them through the Bible and through the teaching of the Church."

When I asked her if she was familiar with the magisterium, she not only gave an accurate definition, but also provided a brief account of how the Church teaches it was formed.

"When Jesus was on earth," Mary Ann began, "He made Peter the rock. From there we have various popes who have come down from him. And we have cardinals, bishops, and priests, down the line. And that's sort of the magisterium of the Church, the governmental hierarchy that watches over us, the shepherds of our Church. From them we learn what Jesus taught. They clarify it for us."

Other Catholics were unable to identify the magisterium.

"The magisterium?" said one man. "Unfamiliar with that."

"I have no idea," answered a Catholic woman.

"Don't know," said Joanne, a teacher in the Rite of Christian Initiation of Adults (RCIA), the Catholic Church's program for adult conversion.

"I've never heard of it," echoed Vera when I asked her what the magisterium was.

"No idea," said Pat.

Most were just as unfamiliar with Tradition.

"I may have heard of that," answered one man in a typical response. "But I can't give you a definition."

All the Catholics with whom I spoke knew about papal infallibility, but when I asked if they personally believed that the pope was immune to error in his official teaching, they were divided.

"No," said Rita. "He's a man. He has his own points of view."

"Nobody's perfect," said Tony.

"I think that he can make errors," a Catholic woman told us. "But I'd really like to believe he's infallible. I know that as a human, though, he can make mistakes."

Other Catholics were confident that the pope could not teach error. Mary Ann was among them. I asked her what she would do if the Bible told her to do one thing but the Church told her to do the opposite.

"I don't think that happens," Mary Ann replied.

"Hypothetically, then?" I asked. "Would you follow the Bible or the Church?"

"I don't think that could happen," she answered, refusing even to consider the possibility.

Richard was willing to consider it, but told me that he would side with Rome.

"I'd stick with the Church," he said, "because of the theological knowledge that the Church has. I'd accept their judgment over my own."

Growing Challenges to Roman Catholic Authority

Though submission to Rome is at the heart of what it means to be a Roman Catholic, don't think for a moment that all Catholics are as compliant as Mary Ann and Richard. Indeed, the Church is finding it increasingly difficult to keep its feisty flock in line. As never before, educated Catholics living in free and pluralistic societies are questioning Rome's teaching on a variety of topics: artificial contraception, divorce, reception of the Eucharist by divorced and remarried Catholics, priestly celibacy, the ordination of women, general absolution, academic freedom for teachers and theologians, and the relationship of national conferences of bishops to the Vatican.

Many Catholics who disagree with the Church's teaching remain in the Church and have no intention of leaving, but remain on their own terms. Sometimes referred to as *cafeteria Catholics,* they accept some aspects of the faith, redefine others, and reject the rest, much like a person passing through a cafeteria line.

Two hotbeds of Catholic discontent are Europe and North America. Some two million Catholics in Germany and Austria recently signed petitions calling for the Vatican to make celibacy for priests optional, to open up the priesthood to women, to support the inclusive treatment of homosexuals, and to recognize a "primacy of conscience" in regard to the use of artificial birth control. Similar petitions are now circulating in the Netherlands, Belgium, Italy, Spain, and France. Once proudly described as the "eldest daughter of the Church," France is now being called Rome's "most rebellious child."

Many European Catholics have stopped listening to the Church altogether. The Vatican's prohibition on the use of artificial birth control is a case in point. Though formally banned by Pope Paul VI in 1968, Catholics continue to use the pill and other devices. Family size is shrinking across the Continent. The lowest birthrates belong to two Catholic countries: Italy (98 percent Catholic) and Spain (95 percent Catholic), both at 1.2 children per couple.

On the other side of the Atlantic, in the United States and Canada, petitions are also circulating, calling for the same changes. And it is not just the laity who are questioning the authority of Rome—many priests and bishops are as well. Some bishops have been openly, though respectfully, critical of Rome's rigid orthodoxy. Tension between these progressive bishops and more traditionally minded ones has become increasingly evident. Leading bishops have become critical of one another. Some have even used the press to wage their battles, much like politicians.

John R. Quinn, retired archbishop of San Francisco and former president of the National Conference of Catholic Bishops, has called for the reform of the papacy. In a major address at Oxford University, Quinn criticized the centralization of power under then-pope John Paul II. Quinn cited, for example, the way the Vatican appoints new bishops. "It is not uncommon," he writes, "for bishops of a province to discover that no candidate they proposed has been accepted for approval. On the other hand, it may happen that candidates whom bishops do not approve at all may be appointed."[90]

Who's in Charge?

Sister Maureen Fiedler, spokesperson for the progressive We Are the Church Coalition, is among those loudly objecting to the Vatican's ever-narrowing definition of acceptable diversity among Catholics. "Who decides what is authentic and acceptable?" she asks. "Who decides what the boundaries will be?"[91] Hoping to have some say in the direction of the Church, her group is among those circulating petitions calling for reform.

Other Catholics are circulating opposing petitions. One championed by Benedictine Father Paul Marx, called "The Real Catholic Petition," asks signers to "lovingly believe and defend every single teaching and doctrine of the Holy Roman Catholic Church, as defined, protected and taught by the Magisterium and the Holy Father." This petition describes Sister Fiedler's We Are the Church Coalition as "an anti-Catholic organization."

An editorial in a national independent Catholic weekly newspaper highlighted the growing intensity of the squabble. Beginning "Holy Father, We Need to Talk," it stated, "The issues will not disappear, and the tragedy is that the Vatican, instead of providing the space and means for conversation, keeps insisting that everyone simply shut up and stop thinking."[92] With battle lines drawn and swords clashing, the late Cardinal Joseph Bernardin of Chicago stepped into the fray, calling for a truce. Bernardin announced the formation of the "Catholic

Common Ground Project." In a document titled "Called to Be Catholic: Church in a Time of Peril," he decried the polarization that was taking place. Bernardin described how "party lines have hardened. A mood of suspicion and acrimony hangs over many of those most active in the church's life; at moments it even seems to have infiltrated the ranks of bishops….Candid discussion is inhibited…proposals are subject to ideological litmus tests."[93] Bernardin, at the time dying of cancer and with only weeks to live, called for dialogue as a path to establishing common ground between the warring factions.

Cardinal Bernard Law, bishop of Boston at the time, immediately labeled the document as having a "fundamental flaw."[94] "The Church already has 'common ground,' "[95] said Law. "It is found in sacred Scripture and Tradition and it is mediated to us through the authoritative and binding teaching of the Magisterium. Dissent from revealed truth or authoritative teaching of the church cannot be 'dialogued' away….The crisis the church is facing can only be adequately addressed by a clarion call to conversion."[96]

What Law means by "conversion" is that troublemakers need to repent and start acting like true Catholics. They must abandon the notion that they can form their own judgments in matters of faith and morals. They need to subjugate their opinions to the official teachings of the Church.

Because I Like It

Despite all the internal squabbling and discontent, Catholics remain Catholic. They may have their doubts. Their attendance at weekly Mass may be sporadic. They may be—and frequently are—critical of their pope, bishops, and priests. They may disagree with the Church's moral teachings. They may wander, sampling other -ologies and -isms. They may even incorporate aspects of other belief systems into their faith. But leave the Catholic Church? Never.

One poll measuring the loyalty of American Catholics found that only six percent had ever seriously thought of leaving the Church. Only two percent said it was likely they would go. In a culture as open to change as the United States, the results were unexpected, proving once again the old axiom: Once a Catholic, always a Catholic.

Most Catholics have never seriously questioned or critically examined the doctrines of Roman Catholicism. They didn't join the Church because of its doctrines, and they don't remain in the Church because of its doctrines. They are Catholic, as they will tell you themselves, because they were born Catholic. They remain Catholic because that's where they feel most comfortable. That's what the people we interviewed outside Saint Joseph's Cathedral told us.

When I asked Vera why she was a Catholic, she answered, "I'm Catholic because I want to be. I was born a Catholic, and I want to be one."

Beatrice, a woman in her sixties, said the same: "Because I want to be. I grew up in a Catholic family. When I was young, I did whatever my parents did. Now that I'm an old person, I enjoy being a Catholic. I never thought of changing my faith. I like being Catholic. I feel comfortable being Catholic."

Andrew Greeley, a Catholic priest of the archdiocese of Chicago and professor of sociology at the University of Arizona, says research has shown that the primary reason Catholics remain Catholic is very simple: "They like being Catholic."[97] Greeley believes that "as an institution the Catholic Church is in terrible condition,"[98] and American Catholics are angry "at the insensitivity and the incompetence of their leaders."[99] Nevertheless, those born Catholic for the most part remain Catholic because overall they like it.

What is it that people like about being Catholic? It's who they are, their personal identity. A booklet edited by Catholic priest Father George R. Szews entitled *Why I Am Catholic: 21 People Give Their Own Answers*[100] demonstrates this.

"I grew up Catholic in a household in which being Catholic simply was part of being," wrote Ron, one of the contributors. "It was a legacy, the same as my name, genetic code, and language." Like many Catholics, Ron thinks of his Catholicism as a matter of his personal destiny. "God wanted me to be Catholic," he wrote, "and that was that."[101]

Kay, a registrar at a Midwestern university, sees her Catholicism in a similar manner. "My Catholic faith seems as essential a part of me as my heart," Kay explained. "Somewhere, somehow, being raised Catholic made me want to remain Catholic, even during those college days when I rebelled against most other establishments."[102]

Others said they were Catholics because in the Church they found the moral framework that they needed for life. It was a place for their children to form proper values and to learn about God. They liked the emphasis in the Church on loving one's neighbor, right living, and social justice. Others spoke of the beauty, inspiration, and peace that the Church brought to their lives.

"Celebrating communion every week is important to me," wrote Ann. "It centers me and gives me the strength I need to accept the grace of God and live up to my values in my daily life."[103]

Several also mentioned that they liked the diversity they find within the Catholic Church. They approved of Rome's willingness to accommodate everything from the traditional, to the contemplative, to handclapping Pentecostalism. They saw the Church as having a healthy mix of different kinds of people, all of whom were welcome. Related to this, others spoke of the sense of community they found within the Church.

"I needed to be part of a real community,"[104] explained one woman.

"Without doubt, the reason I remain Catholic is because of the internal support I have been given during my struggles with life,"[105] wrote a Catholic teacher named Chuck.

Most of the contributors mentioned God in their explanation of why they were Catholic. Ten said that the Church was a place to learn about God, experience His presence, find strength to live right, and to cope with life's trials. Five said God had destined them to be Catholic.

A few also mentioned God in passing in remarks, such as, "God works in strange ways."[106]

The primary reasons the 21 contributors gave for why they were Catholic, however, had little to do with the religious beliefs and practices that distinguish Roman Catholicism from other forms of Christianity. None of the contributors said they were Catholic because they were convinced the Roman Catholic Church was the one, true church instituted by Christ. No one said they were Catholic because the doctrines of Roman Catholicism were true, or because the Church taught what the Scriptures taught. Only five mentioned Christ. Only one—a teacher named Richard—referred to Jesus with any emphasis. He was the only Catholic who spoke of Christ's saving death on the cross or His resurrection. The only other reference even close to Richard's was from a man who said that Christmas and Easter were meaningful to him because of Jesus. Five made no mention of God or Christ.

An Old Shoe that Fits Well

All of this goes to show that doctrine is not important to most Catholics. They didn't join the Church because of doctrine, and they don't stay in the Church because of doctrine. Indeed, many of the reasons the contributors gave for why they were Catholic would have been just as valid for explaining why they belonged to a social service club, such as Rotary International, or an ethnic heritage association, like the National Italian American Foundation.

It also explains why many Catholics are often unaffected by criticism from non-Catholics about the doctrines of Roman Catholicism. Lacking both an interest and a knowledge of Catholic theology, most Catholics simply shrug off such challenges as irrelevant. *Who cares!*

That's what Patricia, a born-again Christian who had left the Catholic Church, experienced when she tried to witness to her Catholic parents. For months she had tried unsuccessfully to help her parents see the difference between Roman Catholicism and biblical Christianity. They refused to discuss the matter or even to look at the Bible with her. Realizing that she wasn't getting anywhere, one day Patricia decided to try a fresh approach. Her plan was to get her parents talking about their religion with the hope of moving the conversation toward the gospel. With that in mind, she struck up a conversation with her father.

"What did you think of Vatican II?" Patricia asked him.

"I didn't know there was another Vatican," her father answered, thinking Vatican II must be the designation of a new second headquarters for the Roman Catholic Church. That was when Patricia realized how little doctrine had to do with her father's loyalty to the Catholic Church. He didn't even have enough interest in the teachings of his Church to know that the most important Catholic event of the last century was the Second Vatican Council, commonly referred to as Vatican II. His Catholicism, she realized then, was just "an old shoe that fits well."

The same is true of most Catholics. They are Catholic because they were born Catholic. They remain Catholic because they like it. Unconcerned about doctrine, they pass through life without ever having seriously questioned the veracity of the institution to which they have entrusted their eternal souls.

How You Can Help

1. Check that your Catholic friend has a Bible that is readable and convenient to use, not an oversized family edition with out-of-date English. Explain how the Bible is organized and how to find a specific passage. Suggest a starting place. The Gospel of John is a good place to begin reading the Bible. Here are some questions you can use when talking to Catholics about God's Word.

   ◆ How much of the New Testament have you read as an adult?

   ◆ What do you think is the main message of the Bible?

   ◆ Have you ever checked the New Testament to see if the practices and doctrines of Roman Catholicism were taught by Christ and His apostles?

2. Encourage your Catholic friend to read the Bible. Avoid criticizing his church or correcting his every observation from the Bible. Give him a chance to get started. Help him to see that with God's help, he can understand the Bible. Once a person seeking God discovers this, there is no stopping him.

3. Make use of the new openness Catholics have toward non-Catholic Christians and invite your Catholic friend to study the Bible or go to a church activity with you. An informal home Bible study is usually the best place to start.

Part Four

Talking to Catholics
About Leaving

13

My Children Are
All Defecting

Dave Sheridan had no idea his life was about to change forever when he returned home from work that evening. As he entered his house, his wife, Barbara, greeted him with her usual smile and a kiss. Then came the first hint that something was up. "Kathleen wants to talk with you," she said. "Alone."

Dave detected a nervous strain in Barbara's voice. Such a formal request from nine-year-old Kathleen, eldest of their three children, was unusual. Realizing the matter must be important, Dave asked Kathleen to join him in his den, offering his daughter a seat in front of his desk.

"What do you want to talk about, Kathleen?" Dave asked.

"Daddy," she said without pretense, "I'm going to heaven."

Kathleen made the announcement so abruptly and with such confidence that Dave could only chuckle in amusement. He had never heard anyone claim such a thing. At the time he was the vice chairman of the parish council, head of a Catholic study group, and a trainer who prepared laity to serve as Eucharistic ministers and lectors. Dave also had helped formulate the baptism and first Holy Communion preparation programs for the parish. Still not feeling like he was doing enough, he had begun attending daily Mass. Yet despite all his learning, service, and participation in the sacraments, Dave didn't know whether he was going to heaven. *She's just a kid,* Dave thought to himself. *What does she know? I'll get to the bottom of this.* "How do you know you're going to heaven, Kathleen?"

"Today I asked Jesus Christ to save me," Kathleen answered without hesitation.

"That's wonderful, honey," Dave replied. *I bet this is something they told her at that club the kids are attending.*

What Kathleen was attending was a vacation Bible club at the local Baptist church. It was a first for the Sheridans. The kids were out of school for the summer. Barbara had run out of activities to keep Kathleen and her two siblings busy. Seeing an advertisement for a children's vacation Bible club in the paper, she had asked Dave if the kids could go. He hesitated when he learned that a Baptist church was sponsoring it, but figuring no harm could be done, gave his consent. Now two weeks later, he was wondering if he had made a mistake. *Ah, she's just a child,* he told himself. "That's fine, Kathleen," he told her.

A few days later, Barbara and the children attended the closing ceremony of the Vacation Bible School. There she met Bill Maupin, pastor of the sponsoring Baptist church. Bill asked Barbara if Kathleen had told her about her decision to trust Christ. When Barbara said she had, Bill asked if he could visit Barbara and her husband in their home sometime to discuss Kathleen's decision. Barbara agreed, and they set up an appointment.

Dave was furious when he learned about the planned visit. "Absolutely not!" he told his wife. Barbara was curious, however, about what the pastor wanted to tell them, so she put off canceling the visit, hoping Dave would change his mind.

When Dave learned that the appointment had yet to be cancelled, he reconsidered. *What am I afraid of? I'm a well-educated Catholic and certainly know more about religion than any Baptist pastor.* "Tell the pastor to come on over," Dave told Barbara. "I'll talk to him."

When Bill Maupin arrived at the Sheridan home, Dave and Barbara welcomed him warmly. The Sheridans were prepared for a rousing discussion about religion. But Bill spoke only about the Lord and what He meant to him. The Sheridans had been around religious people all their lives. They had never heard anyone talk about Jesus as Bill did. After the pastor left, Dave commented to Barbara, "He talks as if he knows Him."

On that first visit, Bill gave Kathleen a workbook called *What Jesus Wants You to Do.* A week later he was back to see how she was getting along. Dave and Barbara enjoyed the visit and invited him back. A friendship developed and, after a time, Bill invited Dave and Barbara to visit the church he pastored, Brecksville Chapel. Dave turned him down. He was Catholic. But since he and his family were going to Saturday evening Mass to keep Sundays free to watch football, Dave told Barbara she and the kids could go if they liked.

The next Sunday, Barbara and her children visited Brecksville Chapel. They returned home excited. The worship was simple and sincere, the Bible teaching clear and practical. Barbara and the kids attended each of the next four weeks, each time returning home more enthusiastic than the time before.

When Dave finally decided that it was time to see for himself what was so special about this church, his initial reaction was shock. Brecksville Chapel wasn't a church at all. It was nothing more than a room at the back of the Clippity Clop Saddle Shop on Route 82! Dave was accustomed to stained-glass sanctuaries and Gothic cathedrals. He couldn't imagine anyone worshiping in a saddle shop! Regardless, even Dave could see that there was something special about the people there. The men especially impressed him. They prayed aloud in their own words and seemed to know the Bible almost as well as the pastor. Dave also found the service interesting, a welcomed change after years at Mass.

As the weeks went by, however, Dave become uncomfortable with the direction his family was heading. His fears were confirmed during one of Bill's visits to the Sheridan home. Colleen, the Sheridans' middle child, announced, "Daddy, I'd like to receive Jesus Christ as my personal Savior!" Colleen was in the second grade, preparing to receive her first Holy Communion. Dave knew, however, that Colleen wasn't referring to receiving Christ at Mass. She was talking like a Baptist!

"She's only seven years old," Dave apologized to Bill. "I don't think she knows what she's asking."

Bill took Colleen's request seriously. He asked her several questions and then carefully reviewed with Colleen the way of salvation. Though her parents couldn't completely follow Bill's explanation, it was clear to them from Colleen's answers that she knew exactly what Bill was talking about. Bill asked Dave and Barbara if they had any objections to Colleen praying to receive Jesus Christ. How could they say no? Colleen and Bill got down on their knees. Dave and Barbara followed. Colleen told God she was a sinner and wanted Jesus to save her.

What's happening to my family? Dave thought to himself as little Colleen prayed. *I've raised these children to be good Catholics. They're all defecting!*

Loyalty to the Church

What should have been a cause of rejoicing for Dave Sheridan was instead a reason for deep concern. There was something un-Catholic about his daughters asking Jesus to save them. Maybe letting them visit the Baptist Church hadn't been such a good idea after all. He knew the Second Vatican Council taught that all Christians are part of the family of God. Yet for Dave there were still two kinds of Christians: Catholics and non-Catholics. And now with two of his children talking like Baptists, Dave was wondering if his family had edged dangerously close to the line that divides.

Crossing that line can mean civil war in a family. Take, for example,

Pilar (named after Nuestra Señora del Pilar, Our Lady of the Pillar), a young woman living in northern Spain. When she told her Catholic parents of her decision to be baptized at an evangelical church, they were furious. They gave her an ultimatum: either stop associating with evangelicals or get out of the house. The next day, they put her and all her possessions out on the street. Pilar phoned a missionary couple who was helping to establish the church in her town and asked them what she should do. They came and got her, welcoming her into their home. Pilar's parents retaliated by picketing the church each Sunday for over a year. They hurled abuses at all who entered and told everyone in the neighborhood that the group was a cult and had kidnapped their daughter.

Another example is what happened to Renae. When she trusted Christ at age 20 and told her parents that she was leaving the Catholic Church, they also became angry, especially her father. First he disowned her, placing her photograph facedown on the living room mantel and cutting her image out of a family portrait. When that didn't bring her back into the Church, he threatened to kill the elders of the evangelical church she had begun to attend.

Renae's boyfriend, Joe, experienced similar family troubles when he informed his parents that he was going to be baptized at the same church. His father told him, "You leave the Church, and, as far as I'm concerned, you no longer exist." After that Joe's father refused to talk to him or acknowledge his presence. After six unbearable months, Joe decided to move out.

Three years later, Joe and Renae married. By then Renae's father had cooled down enough to attend the wedding. By the frown he wore to the ceremony, however, Renae's father made it clear that he did not approve. Joe's father refused to attend. He continued to ignore Joe, Renae, and even their children after they were born. On more than one occasion Joe's father walked away from his grandson, who, with outstretched arms, was seeking to be picked up by his grandfather. It took six years before Joe's father softened and received them back into the family.

The results were just as tragic when a Catholic man, an only son living with his elderly parents in rural Ireland, came to Christ. When he informed his parents of his decision to leave the Church, they warned him harshly and did everything in their power to persuade him to change his mind. The son held fast and in time won his father to the Lord through his godly behavior. The day after his father confessed faith in Christ, his mother donned a traditional widow's gown, black from head to toe. From that day forward, she acknowledged neither the presence of her husband or son, treating them both as dead.

Why do Catholics respond so strongly when one of their family members announces that he or she, in a desire to follow Christ, has chosen another church? Much of the reason has to do with the exalted role of the Church in Roman Catholicism. As the dispenser of the sacraments, the Church claims to be necessary for salvation. Vatican II stated that no one can be saved, who, "knowing that the Catholic Church was founded as necessary by God through Christ, would refuse either to enter it, or to remain in it."[107] Further, the Church says that the pope is the *vicar*, or representative, of Christ on earth. He is also the *pontiff* (from the Latin word *pons*, meaning "bridge"), the high priest of the people of God. In view of these teachings, many Catholics equate God and the Church, as well as salvation and the Church. To reject the Church is to reject God. To reject the Church is to risk damnation.

Loyalty to One's Family Heritage

Often culture rather than theology is the reason family members react so strongly when a loved one joins another church. Born Hispanic, Italian, Polish, French, Filipino, or any one of the other predominately Catholic ethnic groups, Catholicism is "in their blood." It's part of their inherited culture. It shapes not only their beliefs about

God, but the way they see themselves and their worldview. An integral part of their personal and family identity, it's one of the "givens" by which they define themselves. And like one's last name, it's not something a person normally thinks about changing or may change without serious repercussions.

Consider the heartbreak parents experience when a son or daughter announces that he or she has decided to leave the Catholic Church for an evangelical one. Parents feel as if they have failed in the solemn responsibility of passing on their spiritual heritage, one that has been handed down for centuries. They should have done more, prayed more, sacrificed more. They can't help but take their child's decision as a personal rejection. Coupled with this are the feelings of embarrassment and shame as news of the conversion travels through the parish and among the relatives. Finally, there is great loss and disappointment. Sunday mornings the family will be divided, separating to worship at different and sometimes opposing churches. The long-hoped-for wedding in the Catholic Church will never be. Neither will there be the family celebrations as grandchildren are baptized and later receive their first Holy Communion and confirmation. And as life draws to a close, there will be no Catholic funeral or burial in the family plot at the Catholic cemetery. The familiar milestones that have marked the passage of life for generations have been ripped up and carried off.

Loyalty to God

Loyalty is a virtue. We admire those who remain faithful to their country, religion, family, or to an ideal. A traitor is someone who behaves in a disloyal or treacherous manner. Unfortunately, when a born-again Catholic chooses to leave the Church, others often interpret the decision as a rejection of God, family, and culture. But that is not the case. It is a rejection of Rome's false religious system, and that alone. Having concluded from the Scriptures that the Roman Catholic Church is not the church founded by Christ, but rather an apostate form of Christianity, the new believer is trying to be faithful to God. He cannot remain in an institution that teaches a false gospel without being disobedient. His decision is essentially the same as that of the first Christians, who left apostate Judaism. They saw that loyalty to God must supersede loyalty to their nation, family, or religion. Just as Peter told the Jewish high priest, "We must obey God rather than men" (Acts 5:29), so these saved Catholics must obey God rather than the Church of Rome.

Though the new Christian realizes that leaving the Catholic Church will hurt those closest to him, the decision to leave is not a rejection of family. On the contrary, it is only after a person has been born again and regenerated by the Holy Spirit that he can begin to love his family as he ought. As we will see in the next chapter, the new believer feels the pain of leaving as keenly as does his family.

The decision to leave the Church is not a rejection of family, neither is it a rejection of one's culture or ethnic heritage. Though Catholicism tends to intertwine itself into a culture, the two are not inseparable. One does not have to be Catholic to be Italian, Hispanic, or Filipino. Indeed, all traditionally Catholic countries now also have communities of non-Catholic Christians. This is especially true in Latin America, which now has as many regular church-attending Protestants as it does Catholics (though most nonchurchgoers still consider themselves Catholic).

It usually takes time—often several years—before Catholic family members can recover from the initial hurt of a family member's conversion and see beyond it. As the believer lives out his faith, family members begin to see that, far from having rejected God, the convert is highly devoted to God. They take notice as the person puts aside sinful and selfish ways and becomes increasingly Christlike in character. They come to see that, far from having rejected the family, the convert has become more loving, caring, and ready to serve. Only then is a Catholic family willing to reconsider what has happened and the possibility that there may have been matters of principle and truth involved in the convert's decision to leave the Church. Only then are they willing to consider the possibility that maybe the defector is right, and perhaps it is they themselves who are out of step with God.

A Life Change that Changes Lives

That was the process that Tom and Franca went through when Gabriella, their 16-year-old daughter, announced she had trusted Christ and wanted to be baptized. They knew she had been going to a Bible study for high school and college students sponsored by an evangelical church. It concerned them that it wasn't Catholic, but when they saw an improvement in their daughter's sometimes-rebellious attitude, they decided to let her attend. When she said she had been born again and wanted to be baptized, however, they felt they had made a mistake.

I later asked Tom and Franca how they felt when Gabriella first informed them of her decision. "It disturbed me," Franca said, "because in my mind she was already baptized. If that was what was needed to get into heaven, she already had it. I could see no reason to have it done again. I was hurt. I felt she was pulling away from us, that she no longer belonged to our spiritual family."

Tom, Gabriella's father, had a similar reaction. "I really felt lonely," he told me. "I felt I didn't have any more importance in her life. I felt she was leaving us for something else."

Terribly hurt and concerned that their daughter was getting involved with a cult, Tom and Franca forbade her to be baptized. Gabriella asked advice from the Christians at the Bible study she was attending. The leaders there counseled her to wait to be baptized until she was older. During the next four years, Gabriella lived out her faith at home. When she finally decided the time had come for her to obey the Lord by being baptized, the situation had changed. Her example at home had won her parents over. They not only gave their consent, but also accepted an invitation to attend her baptism, bringing Gabriella's two grandmothers along with them. It was the turning point for the family.

"When Gabriella was baptized," Franca now recalls, "she gave a speech, explaining how she had come to the Lord and why she was taking this step. She confessed that she was a sinner. She no longer wanted to live her own way. She wanted to dedicate her life to the Lord Jesus. She said she was grateful to her parents for what they had told her about the Lord. She explained how she had come to know the Lord. I loved it!"

So did her father, Tom. "Gabriella's baptism was one of the greatest days of my life," Tom now says. "I came to understand what it's all about. It's hard for me to explain how I felt that day. It was a joyous day. I learned that I wasn't losing a child; I was gaining her closer to me. I learned that God sent His Son for us. It was the beginning of my own coming to the Lord."

Not long after her baptism, Gabriella's parents began to study the Scriptures. Her brother started attending the youth group at her new church. Two years later, all three trusted Christ, left the Catholic Church, and were baptized.

The gospel of salvation likewise spread through the Sheridan home. It happened the same day little Colleen asked Christ to save her. As soon as she finished her prayer, Bill Maupin, the Baptist pastor, turned to Dave and Barbara and asked, "How about Mom and Dad?"

"We need time to think," Dave told Bill. "All this is pretty new to us. We need time and more information—a lot more information."

Bill suggested that they begin reading the Bible. "What I say about salvation doesn't really matter," he told them. "What does the Bible say? That's the important question."

The next day Barbara purchased Bibles for Dave and herself, and that evening when Dave came home from work, he went to his den and began reading the Gospel of John, the place Bill had suggested for them to start. Barbara took her Bible upstairs to the master bedroom, and also began reading John. When Dave first opened to John's

Gospel, his eyes fell on a promise of the Lord Jesus: "If you continue in My word, then you are truly disciples of Mine; and you will know the truth, and the truth will make you free" (John 8:31-32). He silently offered a prayer to God. *That's what I want, Lord. I want to know the truth.* He turned to the beginning of John's Gospel and read until he came to one of the best-loved verses in the Bible: "For God so loved the world, that He gave His only begotten Son, that whoever believes in Him shall not perish, but have eternal life" (John 3:16). The profound simplicity of the verse grabbed Dave. He stopped, picked up his Bible, and went upstairs to show Barbara. To his astonishment, when he entered the room, she, too, had stopped at John 3:16. "Do you realize that if this verse is true," Dave said to Barbara, "it contradicts everything we know and believe as Catholics?"

The weeks that followed were filled with the excitement of discovery. What they learned seemed too wonderful. As Catholics they had become accustomed to having to earn their way into heaven. Now they were reading that salvation was a free gift from God.

After much discussion, one evening Dave and Barbara got down on their knees, one on each side of their bed. Speaking to God in prayer, they each placed their trust in Christ for salvation. They renounced dependence upon the Catholic Church, the sacraments, and their own good works to get them into heaven. The next day they took their children out of the Catholic school and informed the parish priest of their decision to leave the Church.

14

I Love My Parents

Though there was much to be said, not a word was spoken as Lyne and her mother washed the Saturday evening dishes. Lyne was only 17, yet she was making life-changing decisions—ones that both she and her parents realized might tear their happy family apart. Too fearful to talk about it, they worked in troubled silence.

The tension started with a conversation between Errol, Lyne's boyfriend, and Paul, an acquaintance from Montreal. Paul had been studying Hinduism and other Eastern religions when someone directed him to the Bible and salvation through Christ. Paul repented and believed. He told Errol, a longtime friend. Errol also believed and was born again. And Errol, in turn, told Lyne.

Lyne found the message hard to accept. She was interested when Errol explained God's free offer of salvation. She enjoyed talking with the Christians Errol introduced her to at two small evangelical churches they visited in an adjoining town. But when Errol pointed out the differences between what the Bible said about salvation and what Lyne had been taught in religion classes in Catholic school, she became concerned. When he criticized the Church, she became defensive.

Lyne and her family were Catholics, as was Errol, as was everyone in their village of 4000 in central Quebec, Canada. Catholic missionaries from France—members of orders such as the Society of Jesus (the Jesuits), the Society of Priests of Saint Sulpice (the Sulpicians), and the Ursuline nuns—had helped settle the region in the seventeenth and eighteenth centuries. They had established a Catholic colony governed by a three-man council, permanently reserving one seat for the Catholic bishop. Clergy oversaw all aspects of education, health care, and general welfare. The Jesuits owned much of the land, and laws were passed that banned Protestants from residency.

The Catholic Church no longer retains civil authority in the region. Its influence, however, remains strong. Eighty-six percent of the people in the province of Quebec are practicing Roman Catholics. This province has, by far, the highest concentration of Catholics in any area of Canada or the United States.

Lyne and her family were not just average Catholics; they helped run the parish. Her father was the church sacristan (the custodian in charge of the vestments, sacred utensils, and the sacristy, where the priests prepare before saying Mass). Her mother directed the parish choir. Lyne sang in the choir, served on the parish liturgical committee, and frequently read the Scriptures during the Mass. So when Errol criticized the Church, Lyne's whole way of life was threatened. After three weeks of discussion and debate, the matter came to a head.

"You're destroying everything I believe," Lyne told Errol. "I'm Catholic. I'll never change!"

"You can't remain Catholic," Errol fought back. "There's only one major city in the world built on seven hills—Rome. Revelation 17:9 says the woman who represents false religion in the end times sits on seven hills. You've seen for yourself that the Catholic Church has lied to us. It taught us a false way of salvation. I won't remain Catholic, and neither should you."

Lyne took the Bible from Errol and read Revelation 17 for herself. She saw Errol was right. "There's no other church this chapter could be talking about," she told him reluctantly. "Okay, I'll stop going." She then added, "But I can't bear to face my parents."

Lyne's parents were already on the alert. They knew she and Errol were studying the Bible and talking to evangelicals. "Be careful, Lyne," her mother had warned her. "Errol's new friends are dangerous. They'll brainwash you." Since Lyne was almost an adult, her parents stopped short of forbidding her to talk with them.

During the next few days, Lyne said nothing to her parents about her decision to leave the Church. But by Saturday evening, she knew she could not avoid the issue any longer. The next morning her parents would be expecting her to join them at Mass. Too afraid to speak to her parents directly, she decided to leave a note on the kitchen table. It was brief and to the point. It read: *I won't be going to church tomorrow. Lyne.*

The next morning, Lyne's mother found the note. She called up the stairs to Lyne's bedroom anyway. "Lyne, are you getting up?"

"Sorry, Mother," Lyne answered. "I won't be going to church this morning."

Neither she nor her parents wanted to confront the matter head-on that morning, so nothing further was said. A quiet and uneasy tension set in: Lyne trying to avoid the topic; her parents studying her every expression, trying to figure out what was going on.

The week passed too quickly for Lyne. Soon it was Saturday evening again, and looming over her once more was her parents' expectation that she be at Mass the next morning. As she and her mother washed the dinner dishes at the kitchen sink, Lyne prayed for courage to tell her mother of her decision to leave the Church. Just then the phone rang, and the truth came out under the worst possible circumstances.

"Hello," Lyne's mother said, answering the phone. After a short pause she added, "Oh, hello, Hélène. I'll get her for you."

Lyne's heart sank. Hélène was the woman in charge of organizing the readers for Mass. Lyne was on the rotation. The call was a reminder. She was to read the next morning.

Oh, no! Lyne thought to herself. *Not now!*

"It's for you, Lyne. It's Hélène Laval."

Lyne took the receiver from her mother and, trying to sound casual, greeted the caller. "Good evening, Mrs. Laval."

"Hello, Lyne. I was calling to see if you would read at the nine o'clock Mass."

"No, Mrs. Laval," answered Lyne. With her mother standing beside her and listening to her every word, Lyne didn't want to say more.

"So, you can read at the eleven o'clock Mass?" Mrs. Laval asked.

"No, Mrs. Laval."

"Well, then the five o'clock?"

"No, Mrs. Laval."

"What do you mean? Lyne, you've always been willing to read before."

Lyne tried to find a way out, but it was hopeless. "I won't be going to Mass anymore," she finally blurted out, her eyes on her mother.

"Oh!" Mrs. Laval said, too astonished to say anything else.

"Good-bye, Mrs. Laval," Lyne said, putting down the receiver.

"Do you realize what you're doing?" Lyne's mother asked, her voice trembling with emotion.

"Yes, Mother," Lyne answered. She knew too well. There was no way to soften the blow. She could only watch as her mother broke down in deep sobbing, then retreated to her bedroom in tears. Lyne went to get her Bible and stepped outside on the front porch. Sitting on the steps, she prayed. *Lord, this can't be right. Surely this isn't what You want! It's so hard. I love my parents too much to hurt them like this. I'm willing to do whatever You want, but I'm so confused. Help me, Lord.*

Not knowing where to turn, Lyne opened her Bible. Her eyes fell on counsel from heaven, the words of the Good Shepherd: "Everyone who has left houses or brothers or sisters or father or mother or children or farms for My name's sake, will receive many times as much, and will inherit eternal life" (Matthew 19:29). Lyne then knew what she was doing was right and that God would see her through it. The God of the universe had looked down from heaven, had seen a young French-Canadian girl trying to obey Him, and, from the more than 30,000 verses of the Bible, pointed her to the very one she needed to read.

The months ahead were difficult. Yet Lyne never returned to the Catholic Church or doubted the Lord's direction again.

Saved but Planning to Stay

Earlier we considered how Catholic families react when one of their members decides to leave the Church. Here we will consider the other side of the equation: what the born-again Catholic must face as he or she considers leaving.

The process starts with salvation and the realization that the Catholic Church is wrong. Unlike Lyne, however, most born-again Catholics do not immediately see leaving as a necessary consequence of believing. A young man named Harry comes to mind. A muscular fellow with a bent toward drinking and fighting, Harry couldn't keep out of trouble. His most recent brawl had left him with a broken arm. He went to his parish priest for help but found it ineffective. He looked to friends, and someone pointed him to an evangelical church in his neighborhood. There he met Mike, who took Harry under his care and shared with him the way of salvation. A few days later, Harry professed faith in Christ.

The results were immediate. Harry's aggressive nature was transformed into a zealous enthusiasm for God. In his mind, however, Harry was still Catholic. And so after a few weeks, having found the help for which he had been looking, Harry said good-bye to Mike, telling him he was going back to the Catholic Church.

"How many years have you been in the Catholic Church, Harry?" Mike asked him.

"Twenty-eight."

"How long have you known the Lord?"

"Two weeks."

"Does that tell you anything, Harry?"

Harry got the point. Why return to a church that hadn't been able to help him and hadn't told him the message of salvation?

Other born-again Catholics have an even harder time leaving the

Catholic Church. When encouraged to leave, they instinctively answer, "I was born Catholic, and I'll die Catholic."

"Don't tell me you were born a Catholic," one Filipino Christian is quick to correct those who want to go back. "You were *born* a sinner; you were *baptized* a Catholic." His point is well taken. It doesn't make sense to give your dying allegiance to a religion simply because your family belongs to it. "Had you been born in the southern region of the Philippines," he reminds his friends, "you would have been born a Muslim. Would that mean that Islam is the right religion for you?" It's hard to argue with such unassailable logic.

Still other born-again Catholics, driven by misguided loyalties, remain in the Catholic Church, convinced that, despite its faults, Christ instituted it. They know the Church doesn't preach the gospel. They know the Mass is not what the Church says it is. They know the priest cannot absolve sins. Nevertheless, they remain, thinking Christ is there.

But He's not. He is not in the Eucharist. He is not in the tabernacle of the main altar. He is not hanging on the bigger-than-life crucifix suspended by cables over the altar. Christ does not dwell in buildings, but in the hearts of the redeemed. And where the gospel is not preached, the people remain dead in their sins, void of the life of God. Those looking for Christ in the Church of Rome are looking in a graveyard, even as the women on the day of Jesus' resurrection. The angel asked them, "Why do you seek the living One among the dead?" (Luke 24:5). Good question! As the angel said, "He is not here, but He has risen" (verse 6). Born-again Catholics need to realize the same is true of the Church of Rome. They're looking in the wrong place; Christ is not there.

Staying in Hope of Changing the Church

Some argue that born-again Catholics must remain within the Church if it is ever to change. To leave would be a terrible mistake. All the family friction is unnecessary, they say. Work within the system.

Share with others what you have found. If everyone leaves, how is the Church going to change?

Such advice is both misinformed and unbiblical. Born-again Catholics staying within the Church are not going to change it. Review the history of Roman Catholicism over the past 500 years. That's how long it has been since Luther and others tried to change it. The Church responded with sword and stake. Visit the cities of Europe and stand where Christians were tortured and burned at the stake for their faith. Read the documents of the Council of Trent, Rome's response to its critics. The Council pronounced, "If anyone says that the sinner is justified by faith alone...let him be anathema."[108] Can that be overturned? Can a Church that claims to be infallible change, a Church that turns its errors into dogmas and pronounces solemn judgment on those who say otherwise? Rome has yet to repent of a single error.

Rome is not moving toward the truth, but away. In 1870, at the First Vatican Council, 533 Roman Catholic bishops proclaimed the pope to be infallible, immune to error in his official teaching. This placed the words of a man on the same level as the words of God in inspired Scripture. It also painted the Church into a corner, for now it cannot change or admit a single error.

Some point to the Second Vatican Council (1962–65) as evidence that the Church is improving. They claim that in recent years the Catholic Church has become increasingly evangelical in its outlook. But what has changed? The goal of Vatican II was to update the Church, not to reform it. The Council modernized some practices; refocused the goals of the clergy and laity; refreshed the liturgy, making room for the language of the people to replace Latin at the Mass; and formally expressed the Church's new openness toward both Christians and non-Christians. Most believe these changes were positive. *Vatican II, however, did not change a single dogma of Roman Catholicism.* On the contrary, the Second Vatican Council reemphasized the Church's traditional roots, repeatedly citing in its documents the teachings of the previous 20 councils. It stated: "This sacred council accepts loyally the venerable faith of our ancestors....It proposes again the decrees of the Second Council of Nicea, of the Council of Florence, and of the Council of Trent."[109]

In 1994 the Catholic Church again restated in the *Catechism of the Catholic Church* its commitment to its traditional teachings. The *Catechism*, the Church's first official summary of the faith in some 400 years, cited the Council of Trent 100 times.

Evangelical Catholicism

The recent emergence of an evangelical-looking form of Catholicism in certain countries is presently spawning new claims that Rome is becoming more biblical. But once again the change is only external. The new look is nothing more than old-time Catholicism repackaged to capitalize on the success of the modern evangelical movement. *Nothing has changed.*

Others think Rome must be changing because they have heard of a particular parish where the priest, supposedly having been born again, is preaching the gospel each week at Mass. I've been unable to verify a single case. Occasionally a priest does get saved, but he will not be wearing a Roman collar long if he begins preaching the gospel of grace, refuses to perform the Sacrifice of the Mass, stops leading prayers to Mary, and ceases to hear confession. Even if a number of such born-again priests could be found, with more than 400,000 Roman Catholic priests in the world, would 10, 20, or even 100 born-again priests qualify as a trend? The opposition that these men would be sure to experience from the Church would be a better indicator of the true course on which Rome is sailing.

The Roman Catholic Church has not changed, and it is not about to. Counseling born-again Catholics to remain within the system and work to make a difference is folly. Practically speaking, what is the new Christian supposed to do? Talk to his friends about the Lord? Go see the priest? Write a letter to Rome? Do such actions really have the potential of reforming the Roman Catholic Church?

A Hierarchical Monarchy

The truth is that neither priests nor parishioners have any say in the direction of the Roman Catholic Church. It is not a democracy. It is a hierarchical monarchy. Bishops, some 4700 in number, lead it. The seat of power is the Vatican. From there the pope rules as the supposed vicar of Christ and head of the college of bishops. Aiding the pope are his top advisers and administrators, known as *cardinals*. These oversee the *Roman Curia*—the powerful administrative and judicial offices of the Vatican.

This structure makes no room for democratic change or grassroots movements. It is a top-down organization. Catholics can try to influence the thinking of the hierarchy through letters, petitions, and protests, but none of these means are encouraged or welcomed by the Church.

Even if a significant mechanism for popular change existed, think for a moment what would have to change in order for the Roman Catholic Church to become a biblical church. The pope would have to resign, acknowledging that Christ is the head of the church (Colossians 1:18). The bishops would have to drop their claim to sole teaching authority, recognizing the Holy Spirit as the Church's only infallible and authoritative teacher (John 14:26; 16:13; 1 John 2:27). The Catholic priesthood would have to disband, confessing that the Sacrifice of the Mass is an insult to the finished work of Christ and that no one can forgive sin but God alone (Mark 2:7; Hebrews 10:18). Catholic altars would need to be torn down, confession booths removed, statues destroyed (Exodus 20:4). Veneration and prayer to Mary and the saints would have to stop (1 Timothy 2:5). The Church would have to confess that it has been preaching a false gospel, leading countless millions down the wide path that leads to destruction. It would have to acknowledge that baptism is not the instrument of justification, that its sacraments cannot dispense the grace of God, that eternal life is not a merited reward, and that venial sin, acts of penance, purgatory, and indulgences are the inventions of men. Finally, the

Church would have to begin proclaiming salvation by grace alone through faith alone in Christ alone and, forsaking all dependence upon Tradition, using the Scriptures as its sole guide to truth. None of this is about to happen. And if it did, what would remain would not be the Roman Catholic Church as we know it.

There is no indication that any of this is likely to happen. Neither should we expect God to step in at this late date and revamp the Church of Rome. God is in the business of saving people, not restructuring man-made institutions such as the Roman Catholic Church. We should be in the same business as God.

God's instruction to those who find themselves in apostate churches teaching a false gospel is to get out: "Come out of her, my people, that you will not participate in her sins and receive of her plagues; for her sins have piled up as high as heaven, and God has remembered her iniquities" (Revelation 18:4-5).

For anyone to advise a born-again Catholic to remain in the Church and try to change it is to exhibit an appalling lack of understanding toward the commands of God, the nature of the Roman Catholic Church, and the needs of a new believer. Newly born-again Christians need nurturing and the "pure milk of the word" (1 Peter 2:2), not half-truths, lies, and confusion. They need fellowship with likeminded believers. They need a church in which they can worship God, free of idolatry and false sacrifice.

Staying in Hopes of Reaching Family

Some born-again Catholics, knowing the Catholic Church to be both wrong and impossible to reform, remain nevertheless, hoping to reach unsaved family and friends with the gospel. They believe that if they leave the Church, their family will cut them off and thus their opportunity to influence family members will be lost. But actually the opposite is true. Leaving makes the clearest and strongest statement to family and friends. It is as we separate ourselves from false religion that the difference between truth and error becomes apparent. Separation actually provides the greatest opportunity to reach one's family with the gospel.

Time and again this has proven to be the case. As recounted in the previous chapter, it was through a clear confession of Christ by Gabriella, her departure from the Church, her example at home, and her baptism that her family came to the Lord. Lyne, whose story is told at the beginning of this chapter, has seen her two brothers come to Christ. Harry, mentioned earlier, never did go back to the Catholic Church. Instead his family came to him, visiting his new church in a steady stream. Several members have made professions of faith.

Trying to witness to family and friends from within the Church only confuses the issues. It sends mixed signals. With his lips the born-again Catholic is trying to explain biblical salvation to those around him, but with his life he is telling them that his beliefs are compatible with Roman Catholicism. Should he become openly critical of the Church, his fellow Catholics might rightly ask, "If the Church is so wrong, what are you doing here?"

The Scriptures call us to separate ourselves from false religion:

> Do not be bound together with unbelievers; for what partnership have righteousness and lawlessness, or what fellowship has light with darkness? Or what harmony has Christ with Belial, or what has a believer in common with an unbeliever? Or what agreement has the temple of God with idols? For we are the temple of the living God; just as God said, "I will dwell in them and walk among them; and I will be their God, and they shall be My people. Therefore, come out from their midst and be separate," says the Lord. "And do not touch what is unclean" (2 Corinthians 6:14-17).

What's more, the Lord makes this promise to those who obey:

"I will welcome you. And I will be a father to you, and you shall be sons and daughters to Me," says the Lord Almighty (2 Corinthians 6:17-18).

Family and friends may become angry and critical, but that is part of the cost of being Christ's disciple. The Lord Jesus warned those who would follow Him to expect family troubles:

Do not think that I came to bring peace on the earth; I did not come to bring peace, but a sword. For I came to set a man against his father, and a daughter against her mother, and a daughter-in-law against her mother-in-law; and a man's enemies will be the members of his household (Matthew 10:34-36).

It has never been popular to follow Jesus. Many of the first believers were martyred for their faith. The same is true of hundreds of thousands of believers who, during the time of the Reformation, paid with their lives for refusing to submit to Rome. The Lord Himself was rejected by both His family and His people, being crucified outside of Jerusalem in the company of criminals. He did this for us. God now exhorts us to "go out to Him outside the camp, bearing His reproach" (Hebrews 13:13). This means placing loyalty to Christ above loyalty to family, ethnicity, country, and church. Jesus taught, "He who loves father or mother more than Me is not worthy of Me; and he who loves son or daughter more than Me is not worthy of Me" (Matthew 10:37).

15

The Reformation Is Over!

Keith Fournier is a deacon in the Catholic Church and founder of Catholic Way, an organization that promotes Catholic spirituality. In 1990 he wrote a book entitled *Evangelical Catholics*. In it he called Catholics and Protestants to work together. He wrote, "We must see that we were meant to be one church united under one Head."[110] Charles Colson, founder of Prison Fellowship and popular evangelical author and spokesman, wrote the foreword to the book, stating:

> It's high time that all of us who are Christians come together regardless of the difference of our confessions and our traditions and make common cause to bring Christian values to bear in our society. When the barbarians are scaling the walls, there is no time for petty quarreling in the camp....We have much to forgive, much to relearn.[111]

Colson was aware that evangelical Protestants and Roman Catholics have their differences, but these, at least in his mind, are nothing more than "petty quarreling." Time to forgive, forget, and work together.

Colson continued this theme in his 1992 religious bestseller, *The Body*. There he wrote:

> In recent decades, Catholic and Protestant doctrine has dramatically converged. In the fall of 1991, Pope John Paul II and Lutheran bishops from Scandinavia joined in an ecumenical celebration—not ignoring differences, but emphasizing growing unity on matters of orthodoxy, including justification. In his message, the Swedish primate said: "Dialogue has proven the existence of a basic unity for instance in the question of justification by faith, to which the pope agreed that both sides were 'very close' to a common understanding."[112]

Lutherans and Catholics very close to a common understanding of justification! Who would have thought? Colson, however, was correct, as we will see.

Unity at the Expense of Truth

Evangelicals and Catholics Together (1994)

Evangelical Christians should have been shocked by the ecumenical thrust of *The Body*. Instead, the book became a bestseller. Even Colson was unprepared for *The Body's* widespread acceptance, commenting, "That reflection on biblical themes of the Church and unity in Christ captured the evangelical imagination, strengthening our intuition that the time had come to take the initiative that would eventually produce ECT."[113]

What Charles Colson means by ECT is "Evangelicals and Catholics Together," the 1994 ecumenical accord spearheaded by him and Roman Catholic priest Richard John Neuhaus, a former Lutheran minister who converted to Roman Catholicism. In this document, evangelical and Catholic signers apologized for past hostilities: "We together, Evangelicals and Catholics, confess our sins against the unity that Christ intends for all his disciples." Together they declared their unity: "Evangelicals and Catholics are brothers and sisters in Christ." The signers promised to refrain from further hostilities and from evangelizing one another's flocks, labeling such activity "sheep stealing." They pledged to work together and to witness together that through united action they might prepare the world for the second coming of Christ. Among those joining Charles Colson in signing ECT were evangelicals J.I. Packer (Regent College), Bill Bright (Campus Crusade for Christ), Pat Robertson (Regent University), Os Guinness (Trinity Forum), Richard Mouw (Fuller Theological Seminary), and Mark Noll (Wheaton College). The document and a complete list of Catholic and evangelical signers is available at the website of First Things (www.firstthings.com).

Other well-known evangelicals were outraged. John MacArthur called upon the evangelical signers to recant. R.C. Sproul, James Kennedy, John Ankerberg, and others strongly criticized the document. Dave Hunt called "Evangelicals and Catholics Together" a betrayal of the Reformation.

Responding to growing criticism, J.I. Packer wrote a defense of ECT. *Christianity Today* published it in its December 1994 edition. Entitled "Why I Signed It," Packer argued in the article, "Do we recognize that good evangelical Protestants and good Roman Catholics— good, I mean, in terms of their own church's stated ideal of spiritual life—are Christians together? We ought to recognize this, for it is true."[114]

What it means to be a "good Roman Catholic" is defined in the *Catechism of the Catholic Church.* There you will find a false gospel of infant baptismal justification, good works and sacraments necessary for salvation, a merit system whereby Catholics working in cooperation with grace can earn eternal life, and a reaffirmation of purgatory as a place where Catholics atone for their sins. These beliefs describe Rome's ideal of spiritual life.

Undaunted by criticism and rebuke, Colson wrote the following year, "We are regularly asked whether we are pleased with the response to ECT. Pleased is not the word for it. We are immeasurably grateful to

God for what he has done and continues to do through this initiative."[115] The evangelicals associated with Colson hope to form even closer ties with Catholics. He writes, "Our work is far from done. As we said, ECT is only a beginning. We do believe this effort has been blessed by God, and we are gratified beyond measure by the reception it has received from innumerable evangelical and Catholic Christians."[116]

J.I. Packer believes Catholic/evangelical unity is already a reality. He points to shared worship services and to joint efforts on social issues, such as opposition to abortion. He writes:

> Billy Graham's cooperative evangelism, in which all the churches in an area, of whatever stripe, are invited to share, is well established on today's Christian scene. And so are charismatic get-togethers, some of them one-off, some of them regular, and some of them huge, where the distinction between Protestant and Catholic vanishes in a Christ-centered unity of experience.[117]

Packer concludes, "So the togetherness that ECT pleads for has already begun. ECT, then, must be viewed as fuel for a fire that is already alight."[118]

How does the pope and Rome's claim to being the one, holy, catholic, and apostolic church instituted by Christ fit into this growing fraternity of Catholics and Protestants? Packer thinks just fine: "In the days when Rome seemed to aim at political control of all Christendom and the death of Protestant churches, such partnership was not possible. But those days are past and after Vatican II can hardly return."[119]

Packer is right in saying ecumenical unity is becoming a reality. But as to the ambitions of Rome in joining hands with evangelicals, he is mistaken. The Catholic Church has never dropped its claim to the "control of all Christendom." In its recently released *Catechism of the Catholic Church*, the Vatican states, "For the Roman Pontiff, by reason of his office as Vicar of Christ, and as pastor of the entire Church has full, supreme, and universal power over the whole Church, a power which he can always exercise unhindered."[120] In its "Decree on Ecumenism," the Second Vatican Council unabashedly stated that its goal in working toward unity is that all would return to the Roman Catholic Church:

> The results will be that, little by little, as the obstacles to perfect ecclesiastical communion are overcome, all Christians will be gathered, in a common celebration of the Eucharist, into the unity of the one and only Church, which Christ bestowed on his Church from the beginning. This unity, we believe, subsists in the Catholic Church as something she can never lose, and we hope that it will continue to increase until the end of time.[121]

Lutherans and Catholics Together (1999)

Lutherans are also joining hands with Rome. For some 35 years the Lutheran World Federation (LWF) has been having official talks with the Roman Catholic Church in an effort to overcome their differences. They reached a significant milestone on October 31, 1999, when in Augsburg, Germany, the two parties signed a document entitled "The Joint Declaration on the Doctrine of Justification by the Lutheran World Federation and the Catholic Church." Signing for the LWF was its president, Lutheran bishop Christian Krause. Signing for the Roman Catholic Church was Cardinal Edward Cassidy, president of the Pontifical Council for Promoting Christian Unity.

The Lutheran World Federation (LWF) is the largest international communion of Lutheran churches. Founded in 1947, it is headquartered in Geneva, Switzerland. It has 138 member churches in 77 countries and represents 65 million Lutherans. This is most, though not all, of the world's Lutherans. (The Missouri Synod, for example, is not part of the LWF.) The LWF works closely with the World Council of Churches (WCC), an organization that describes itself as "the broadest and most inclusive among the many organized expressions of the modern ecumenical movement, a movement whose goal is Christian unity."[122] The WCC brings together more than 340 churches and represents some 400 million people within various Christian denominations. Though not an official member of the WCC, the Roman Catholic Church works closely with the organization and participates in many of its ecumenical efforts.

The 1999 "Joint Declaration on the Doctrine of Justification" between Lutherans and Catholics was historically significant, bringing together two groups that had been diametrically opposed on the doctrine of justification. Luther held to justification by faith. He saw justification as the declaration of God by which He puts His own righteousness to the account of the person who believes. The Lutheran Augsburg Confession of 1530 states,

> Men cannot be justified before God by their own strength, merits, or works, but are freely justified for Christ's sake, through faith, when they believe that they are received into favor, and that their sins are forgiven for Christ's sake, who, by His death, has made satisfaction for our sins. This faith God imputes for righteousness in His sight.[123]

The Roman Catholic Church condemned this Lutheran belief at the Council of Trent (1545–1563) and restated the Catholic position as follows:

> To those who work well right to the end and keep their trust in God, eternal life should be held out, both as a grace promised in his mercy through Jesus Christ to the children of God, and as a reward to be faithfully bestowed, on the promise of God himself, for their good works and merits.[124]

Trent defined justification as "a transition from that state in which a person is born as a child of the first Adam to the state of grace and of adoption as children of God through the agency of the second Adam,

Jesus Christ our savior."[125] This is accomplished in Roman Catholicism through the sacrament of baptism.

Despite their great historical differences, in 1999 the Lutherans and Catholics announced that we are "now able to articulate a common understanding of our justification by God's grace through faith in Christ." Before joining the celebration, however, you should read the document. It is available at the Lutheran World Federation website (www.lutheranworld.org) and at the Vatican website (www.vatican.va). You should note that neither side admitted it had been wrong or had changed its position. Half of the 4600-word document is an explanation of their common understanding of justification. It is divided into seven parts. Each has three paragraphs. The first paragraph in each section introduces an aspect of their common understanding and summarizes it in broad terms. These opening paragraphs typically begin, "We confess together that…." The second paragraph states the Catholic understanding of the matter, typically beginning, "The Catholic understanding of this also includes…." The third paragraph states the Lutheran position, typically beginning, "The Lutheran view of this emphasizes…." (The Catholics and the Lutherans take turns going second and third to keep things even.) Had they truly reached agreement, one would think they would have stated their common understanding of justification in the same paragraph. That, of course, would have required one side to admit that it had been wrong and had changed.

Events leading up to the signing of the "Joint Declaration" also indicate there was no true agreement. The Lutherans were first to ratify the document. That took place in June 1998 in Geneva. Almost immediately the Vatican announced that it was having second thoughts, issuing a document on July 9, 1998, entitled "The Response of the Catholic Church to the Joint Declaration." The "Response of the Catholic Church" is also available on the aforementioned Lutheran and Vatican websites and is interesting reading. It restates the Catholic position on justification from the Council of Trent, stating, "We can therefore say that eternal life is, at one and the same time, grace and the reward given by God for good works and merits…." If you read the "Joint Declaration," you'll see why the Vatican felt the "Response of the Catholic Church" was necessary. In the "Joint Declaration," both parties were to agree that "as sinners our new life is solely due to the forgiving and renewing mercy that God imparts as a gift and we receive in faith, and never can merit in any way." Oops! Apparently the Catholic framers of the "Joint Declaration" gave away too much to the Lutherans. Now the Vatican had to get it back again. Upon reading the "Response," one of the Lutheran theologians involved in the project was heard to say it was the darkest day of his life. The previous 30 years of dialogue, he said, were for nothing.

All was not lost, however, for then-Cardinal Joseph Ratzinger, prefect of the powerful Congregation for the Doctrine of Faith and guardian of orthodoxy, took over. On November 3, 1998, he met in private session with Lutheran bishop Johannes Hanselmann and two theologians, one Catholic and one Lutheran. They met at the home of Georg Ratzinger, the cardinal's brother, in Regensburg, Bavaria, and hammered out a solution. The result was a third document, an "Official Common Statement," and then an "Annex to the Official Common Statement," together another 1600 words of "elucidations," describing the consensus the two parties had reached. These are also available on the Lutheran and Catholic websites.

If none of this sounds like true agreement to you, be assured you are not alone. Remember, it took more than 30 years to write the document. That alone should tell you something, and even when it was finished, both sides had trouble agreeing that they had agreed. The document itself is a masterpiece of equivocation—the use of vague and ambiguous language for the purpose of obscuring the truth. Apparently both Lutheran and Catholic leadership were determined not to let doctrine keep them from unity. With justification no longer separating them, they can now move forward on other fronts. Lutheran leader Bishop Johannes Friedrich of Bavaria has since said that the papacy "does not have to constitute, in the future, an element of separation between Catholics and Protestants."[126] He was reported in the Catholic press as saying "he could envision the role for the Catholic pontiff as 'spokesperson' for all Christians in a globalized world."[127]

The Eleventh Annual Wheaton Theology Conference (2002)

A final indication of the growing unity with Catholics was provided by Wheaton College in 2002. Perhaps the best-known evangelical liberal arts college in America, when its theology department convened the eleventh annual Wheaton Theology Conference, it chose as the theme "Catholics and Evangelicals in Conversation." Among the keynote speakers was His Eminence Francis Cardinal George, archbishop of the Chicago Archdiocese. Also headlining the event were ECT signers J.I. Packer, Father Richard John Neuhaus, and Mark Noll, professor of history at Wheaton College. This was not a conference to discuss the barriers to Catholic and evangelical unity, but to explore how to move forward now that they had been removed. Mark Noll reviewed how Catholics and evangelicals are already working together in Billy Graham crusades, the Catholic Charismatic renewal, the anti-abortion movement, and mission groups such as Youth With a Mission (YWAM). Remaining differences, he said, are "trivial." He announced, "The Reformation is over!" As a gesture of goodwill, an offering was taken for a Catholic parish facing financial difficulties.

Mimicking the Truth

Has the leopard changed his spots? Hardly. The Roman Catholic Church has not changed a single doctrine. Rather, as Catholic theologians describe it, the Church has been *reformulating* its answers. There's a new look, but that's all that's happened. Bible-believing Christians should not be fooled. The Scriptures warn that in the end times the greatest threat to the truth will come not from hostile, atheistic governments, but from false teachers claiming to be Christians (1 Timothy 4:13; 2 Timothy 3:19; 2 Peter 2:13). These teachers will "secretly introduce destructive heresies" (2 Peter 2:1) into the true church. It will be a time of apostasy in which "some will fall away from the faith" (1 Timothy 4:1). The tactic these false teachers will use will be an old and familiar one: "Just as Jannes and Jambres opposed Moses, so these men also oppose the truth, men of depraved mind, rejected in regard to the faith" (2 Timothy 3:8). Jannes and Jambres were the magicians who kept Pharaoh from listening to Moses. When Moses threw down his staff before Pharaoh and it became a serpent, the magicians of Egypt "did the same with their secret arts" (Exodus 7:11). The same thing happened when Moses turned water into blood and when he brought frogs upon the land (Exodus 7:20-22; 8:5-7). The magicians did what Moses did. Pharaoh, seeing no difference between Moses and his court magicians, refused to listen to Moses.

Scripture says that "just as" the magicians opposed Moses, "so" the false teachers of the last days will oppose the truth. They will use the same method: mimicry. They will not be atheists who proclaim that God is dead. They will not be enemies of religion who burn Bibles and imprison Christians. On the contrary, they will carry large Bibles and quote them freely. They will talk of God, salvation, grace, truth, and unity. Outwardly they will hold to "a form of godliness" (2 Timothy 3:5), but inwardly deny its power.

The outcome of these false teachers is also predicted in the Bible: "They will not make further progress; for their folly will be obvious to all, just as Jannes's and Jambres's folly was also" (2 Timothy 3:9). Jannes and Jambres were able to mimic Moses' first three signs, but they failed to duplicate the fourth. When Moses told Aaron to strike the earth with his staff, "all the dust of the earth became gnats through all the land of Egypt" (Exodus 8:17). Scripture says that the "magicians tried with their secret arts to bring forth gnats, but they could not" (verse 18). Jannes and Jambres confessed, in their failure, "This is the finger of God" (verse 19).

Similarly, the Roman Catholic Church can imitate true Christianity, but only so far. Its false gospel cannot bring forth genuine spiritual life from dead sinners. In a future day, its folly will become obvious to all, even as the folly of the two magicians was exposed.

16

Will I Be Excommunicated?

The following letter received from a young Catholic named Marnie illustrates how difficult it is for a person to leave the Catholic Church.

Dear Mr. McCarthy,

I am an eighteen-year-old senior in high school and reading your book *The Gospel According to Rome.* I was confirmed into the Catholic Church early last summer. I now wish that I had given it more thought. I wish that I had known what I know now about what the Catholic Church stands for and believes in.

While I was going through confirmation class, the teachers stressed that we needed to be sure we would continue to follow and be part of the Church before we were confirmed. At the time I trusted completely in the Church and thought I would spend the rest of my life as a member of it. When non-Catholic friends and acquaintances would argue with me about the Church, I would always defend it. I now realize that I had done this in blind faith.

A few months ago a very good friend of mine made a point about the Church which I couldn't defend. That was the first thing said to me against the Catholic Church that I couldn't argue. This point bothered me for several weeks, until I finally asked the director of religious education at my church about it. I have always been very close to her, and she gave me an answer that sounded reasonable. She also gave me a book containing the Second Vatican Council documents. I started reading it that very night, thinking that it would make me, once again, confident in my faith and in the Church. It did the very opposite.

As I read, I started to realize how ridiculous most of it was. The Catholic Church has a rule for everything. I also noticed that the book was larger than the Bible. Isn't Christianity following what the Bible says? But Catholics must follow what the Church says. Through this time I have also been talking with my friend. He is a person I trust a lot and whose opinion I value. He is a member of a local Bible church which fellow students in my religious education class have cruelly nicknamed "The Psycho Bible Barn." I don't see the humor in it, and don't see how a church that follows the Bible could be "psycho." Also, leaders in my church like to talk about other churches of its kind as if what they do and believe is wrong, all the while believing they are being ecumenically correct by referring to them as "fundamentalist" churches.

I know I cannot continue being a member of the Roman Catholic Church, but I am very scared of the results. My family is mostly all Catholic and would be shocked if they knew what I am contemplating. How does one leave the Church? Is it a formal termination, or do I just stop going to Mass? Will I be excommunicated? How did your family react when you left the Church?

Sincerely,

Marnie

Marnie ended her letter with questions faced by every Catholic who contemplates leaving the Church. My hope in providing the following answers to Marnie's questions is that they might help other

Catholics who are in the process of leaving the Church and those assisting them.

How does one leave the Church? Is it a formal termination or do I just stop going to Mass?

Most born-again Catholics just stop going to Mass, not wanting to cause a fuss. With the pastoral staff of many parishes understaffed and overburdened, it is unlikely that one person leaving will even be missed. Four years after I left the Catholic Church, I was still receiving Easter offering envelopes in the mail from my last parish. It is not unusual for neighborhood churches to operate with a ratio of 2000 or more parishioners to one priest. In some dioceses, there is not even one priest per parish.

When adults leave the Church, it is usually best for them to talk to the parish priest and inform him of the decision. Most priests work hard and deserve the courtesy of a visit. The person leaving should be ready to explain why he is leaving, stating his reasons with biblical support. This also provides the opportunity of being a witness for Christ to the priest. If the new believer does not feel strong enough to speak to the priest alone, he should take someone with him who knows the Bible well and will be able to answer objections.

Will I be excommunicated?

It's unlikely a Catholic leaving the Church will be formally excommunicated. I've never heard of the modern-day Church excommunicating a lay Catholic. I doubt a bishop would even consider it in the case of a person leaving the Catholic Church for another church.

The Church does still excommunicate people, but they are almost always priests or theologians whose public teachings require a public response. The last case I am familiar with was Oblate Father Tissa Balasuriya of Sri Lanka. An outspoken theologian, he disagreed with the Vatican on a number of doctrines. Among them was papal authority—an offense the Vatican will not tolerate. After four years of warnings, the Vatican said Balasuriya had essentially excommunicated himself by his refusal to submit to Rome. Church law states that "an apostate from the faith, a heretic or a schismatic incurs automatic excommunication."[128]

How did your family react when you left the Church?

Marnie asked this question to gauge what might happen in her family upon her leaving the Church. It is usually the hardest issue with which a born-again Catholic has to deal. Such Catholics need prayer and support. Those cut off from their family, even if for only a time, can feel terribly alone.

When I told my parents that I was leaving the Catholic Church, they became very upset. Both had immigrated as adults to the United States from Ireland, and Catholicism was all they knew. To have their eldest son reject their faith was a terrible blow to them. My dad became angry and stormed out of the house. He refused to return until I had left. My mother broke down in tears. My decision created considerable grief for my brothers and sisters as well.

My dad remained upset the longest, including a three-year stretch during which he refused to see me or talk to me. At length, however, we were reconciled. In the final months of his life, I was able to speak to him about the Lord and the biblical way of salvation. He listened, but being a very private man, kept his thoughts to himself. The Lord knew his heart.

My mom passed away several years before my dad. When I first trusted Christ, she and I had several good discussions. These became strained, however, when I left the Catholic Church. Eventually she refused to talk to me about anything spiritual. I continued, however, to give her the occasional book or audiotape, which she would receive with little comment. A few years later she developed cancer and her health declined quickly.

Two months before my mom died, my wife, Jean, and three of my sisters were with her. She told them, "You know, girls, Jean and I have our differences about what we believe, but what's most important is that we both believe that Jesus Christ died for our sins, and that He was buried, and that He rose again."

Jean sensed something had changed. In a family that had been torn apart by the gospel, my mother, who had always been the spiritual mainstay of our family, was saying she was in basic agreement with Jean and me. In addition, in her listing of what was "most important," there was no mention of good works, receiving the sacraments, or going to Mass.

I was surprised when I learned about what my mother had said, but only cautiously optimistic. All Catholics believe that Jesus died for our sins, was buried, and rose on the third day. As we have seen, that doesn't mean they're trusting Christ for salvation. Nevertheless, Jean encouraged me to talk to her about it. "She sounded different," Jean said.

I was hesitant. The subject had long been taboo. But at Jean's prompting, I looked for an opportunity to speak with my mom alone. When it came, I found her open and wanting to talk about the Lord. She was weak and lengthy discussion was not possible, but I went away encouraged, though still unsure whether she was saved.

A few days later, Jean and I had another opportunity to speak with my mother. She asked us to encourage my brothers and sisters to read the Scriptures. She requested a supply of Bibles so she could give them to family and friends. She dictated a list of two dozen names and short inscriptions she asked us to write in each Bible.

With each passing day, it became more evident that my mother had had a spiritual awakening. What I didn't know at the time—only learning after her death while arranging some of her things—was that during those years she had refused to talk with me she had become a serious student of the Bible. Unknown to me, she had read everything I had given her, underlining important passages and completing a correspondence course called *What the Bible Teaches.* She had written summaries of large portions of the Scriptures in a notebook and had marked important passages in her Bible. I was unaware of any of this until after her death, so even after my mother asked us to buy her a supply of Bibles, I still wasn't sure she had been born again.

As her health continued to decline, family members made their final visits. One was a Catholic priest, a cousin of hers. She asked him, "Father, if we're forgiven our sins because of the cross, why do we still have to confess them in the sacrament of penance?" I was shocked. Was my mother really saved? Was she beginning to see the contradictions within Roman Catholicism?

About that time I received the confirmation of her salvation for which I had been hoping. She wrote a prayer on the back of an envelope she wanted my dad to read. Though very weak at the time, she got out of bed and taped it to his shaving mirror. When I read the prayer, I knew her faith was in Christ alone to save her. It read:

> Lord Jesus! I need You. Thank You for dying on the cross for my sins. I open the door of my life and receive You as my Savior and Lord. Thank You for forgiving my sins. Take control of my life. Make me the kind of person You want me to be.

She went to be with her Lord a few days later.

How You Can Help

1. Discussing doctrinal differences with Catholics has its place, but it's not a good place to start. Remember, most didn't become Catholics because of doctrine and they don't remain Catholics because of doctrine. They're Catholics because they like it. It's who they are. So what can you do? Here are some questions you can ask your Catholic friends to get them thinking:

   - Why are you Catholic?

   - In what ways has the Catholic Church helped you spiritually?

   - Have the sex scandals involving priests caused you to reconsider your membership in the Catholic Church?

   - If you were to die tonight, do you think you would go to heaven?

2. Since Catholicism tends to run along family and ethnic lines, many Catholics do not have a single non-Catholic Christian friend. Ask God to increase your love and compassion for Catholics. Then look for ways to nurture friendships with them. You will find that your greatest opportunities to share your faith usually come early in a new relationship, so don't let them pass.

3. Pray in faith, knowing that God loves to save families. The gospel of salvation came to Cornelius and his household (Acts 11:14). The same was true of Lydia (Acts 16:15), the Philippian jailer (Acts 16:31), Crispus (Acts 18:8), Aristobulus (Acts 16:10), Narcissus (Acts 16:11), Stephanus (1 Corinthians 1:6), and Onesiphorus (2 Timothy 4). In the Old Testament we find many believing families, including those of Moses, Hannah, and David. We also find multigenerational faith. The four

generations of Joash, Amaziah, Azariah, and Jotham are one example. Likewise, in the New Testament we find believing families. In Bethany there is Mary, Martha, and Lazarus. In Jerusalem there is Mary, her son John Mark, and her brother Barnabas. In Capernaum there is Zebedee and Salome and their sons Peter and Andrew. In Nazareth there is the Lord's own family—His mother Mary, his half-brothers James and Jude, his cousin Elizabeth, and Elizabeth's son, John the Baptist. The same is true today. The gospel spreads through families. Pray that it might be so in yours, knowing that God loves to save families. When trying to help Catholic family members see the truth, never forget that how you live the Christian life before them will communicate more than what you say to them.

4. Though you should not begin with criticism, don't be paralyzed by the fear of offending your Catholic friend. If the love of God abides within us, we cannot sit by idly while people go unwarned to a Christless eternity. Take the initiative and say something. But remember, if you criticize a person's church, they will usually defend it. Yet if you ask them about their church, they often criticize it themselves. You might also consider giving the person a book or video about Catholicism. When doing so, try one of these approaches.

- When speaking to a devout Catholic: "I know you take your faith seriously. Recently I came upon a book that is fairly critical of Roman Catholicism. Would you be willing to take a look at it and let me know if what the author is saying about Catholic doctrine is true?"

- When speaking to a lapsed Catholic: "Why is it that you don't go to Mass?" Listen to the person's reason, then add, "Would you be interested in a book that explains, from the Bible, why Catholicism doesn't work for so many people?"

- ◆ When speaking to a Catholic family member: "I know it was hard on our family when I left the Catholic Church. I've tried to explain my reasons for leaving, but I'm not sure I've succeeded. Recently I found a book that does a better job of it. I'd like you to have a copy. I hope it helps you to better understand what I've been going through spiritually. I really want us to remain close as a family."

5. If you are a former Catholic, realize that God has uniquely positioned you within a network of friends and family. These relationships are an important part of who you are. They have taken a lifetime to form and have roots generations deep. Cherish and nurture those relationships. Though you are now a new person in Christ, you are still your parents' son or daughter, your siblings' brother or sister, the childhood companion of your friends in the neighborhood. How they will now treat you depends largely on you. If you think of yourself now as an outsider or even an outcast, your actions will soon make it so. *They're all talking about me. I no longer belong. These are not my people.* Such attitudes can only distance you from the very people whom Christ would have you reach for Him.

Instead, decide from the beginning of your new relationship with Christ that you are going to love your Catholic friends and family as never before, regardless of what they think of you or how they treat you. Scripture instructs us, "If possible, so far as it depends on you, be at peace with all men" (Romans 12:18). Commit yourself to being Christ's ambassador to them. Visit them regularly. As you are able, participate in every birthday party, anniversary, and Christmas celebration. Help them through the crises they face. Pray with them when things are hard. Don't allow overactivity in your new church to crowd them out of your life. Rather, bring the new life you have in Christ into your existing relationships. Invest your life in your friends and family, and patiently await God's prompting as to when to speak to them about the Lord. It will come in His time.

6. Avoid developing an adversarial mindset toward devout Catholics, especially priests and nuns. They are not the enemy, but men and women for whom Christ died. Most are sincere and unaware that they follow a false form of Christianity. In the words of Scripture, they are "deceiving and being deceived" (2 Timothy 3:13). A recent trip to Italy comes to mind. I was visiting a small evangelical church outside Rome. The members were local people who had grown up in the Catholic Church. When I suggested to some of the men that we visit the parish priest, they were shocked. Though they all knew the priest, they kept their distance from him, thinking of him as the representative of all that was wrong with Christianity in Italy.

At length, two of the men joined me for the visit. The parish priest welcomed us into his living quarters and had coffee served for us. Two other priests joined us. We had a pleasant conversation. At its conclusion an hour later, I presented each of the priests with a copy of my book *Letters Between a Catholic and an Evangelical,* which they accepted graciously and promised to read. They told us they were Franciscans and invited me to visit their center in Assisi, Italy, and spend a few days as their guest. After we left, my Italian hosts told me they were surprised by the warm reception we had received. They had also come to realize that more could be accomplished by being friendly and reaching out to these priests in the love of Christ than could be done by shunning them. They promised to visit them again.

7. The better you understand Roman Catholicism, the better you will be able to effectively communicate the gospel to Catholics.

Purchase a simple catechism and study it carefully. A good one is *A Catechism for Adults* by Rev. William J. Cogan (Youngstown: Cogan Productions, 1990). Another useful tool is a small Catholic dictionary. The one I like best is the *Pocket Catholic Dictionary* by John A. Hardon (New York: Image Books, 1985). An effective way to keep current on the Roman Catholic faith is to subscribe to a Catholic periodical. If you want to understand the American scene from a conservative perspective, subscribe to *Our Sunday Visitor* (www.osv.com). If you want a progressive viewpoint of the Church internationally and in America, consider an independent newsweekly such as the *National Catholic Reporter* (www.natcath.com). For local Catholic news, subscribe to the official paper of your Catholic diocese. If you want the Church's official position, subscribe to its international weekly newspaper *L'Osservatore Romano* (see www.vatican.va).

And the most useful aid to understanding Catholicism is the *Catechism of the Catholic Church.* It is the official summary of the Catholic faith produced by the Vatican. It's available in bookstores everywhere. It's also accessible online at the Vatican's website (www.vatican.va.). Appendix B provides a doctrinal index to the *Catechism of the Catholic Church,* and this doctrinal index is cross-referenced to my book *The Gospel According to Rome.*

Appendix A

Cards for Sharing the Gospel with Catholics—see Chapter 6, "What Must I Do to be Saved?" for instructions on how to use the cards.

1. BELIEVING AND LOVING GOD

2. BEING BAPTIZED

✂ Cut along outside edge.

3. GOING TO MASS AND RECEIVING THE SACRAMENTS

4. LOVING YOUR NEIGHBOR

5. OBEYING THE TEN COMMANDMENTS

6. DOING GOOD WORKS

7. PRAYING AND
DEVOTION
TO MARY

8. DYING WITH
NO UNCONFESSED
MORTAL SIN

9. ANYTHING
ELSE

10. TRUSTING
JESUS
AS SAVIOR

Appendix B

Doctrinal Index to the *Catechism of the Catholic Church*

Topic	Catechism of the Catholic Church (paragraph numbers)	The Gospel According to Rome (page numbers)
Act of Contrition	1430-39, 1451-54, 1492	73, 77
Acts of penance	1434-39, 1450-60, 1494	78-79, 83
Actual grace	2000, 2024	38, 56-57
Adoration of the Eucharist	1178, 1183, 1378-81, 1418, 2691	131-32, 143-44
Assumption of Mary	966, 974	188, 197, 203, 224, 281-84, 293-300
Attendance at Mass obligatory	1389, 1417, 2042, 2181	131
Baptism	403, 977, 1212-84, 1992, 2020	21-34, 323-32
Bible study	85, 100-41, 2653	276-80, 285-86, 301-03,
Bishops	880-96	234-35, 248-52
Ecumenism	817-22, 855	319-20
Grace by performance of a rite	1127-29	32, 64, 157-58
Grace lost through mortal sin	1033, 1855, 1874	75-76
Hail Mary	435, 2676-78	79, 206, 215
Hierarchical monarchy	771, 779, 880-87	234-61
Immaculate Conception	411, 490-93, 508	186-87, 196-97
Indulgences	1471-79, 1498	94-95, 206
Infallibility	889-92, 2032-35, 2051	79, 206, 215
Initial sanctifying grace	1262-74	26-28, 45-46, 55, 60, 112
Last Rites	1499-1532	89-91, 335
Liturgy and rites	1066-75, 1124-25	17-18, 236
Magisterium	77, 85-88, 100, 113, 861-62, 888-92, 2032-40, 2049-51	263-80
Mary	273, 411, 484-511, 618, 721-26, 773, 829, 963-75, 2030, 2617-19, 2622, 2673-82	95, 181-230, 293-300
Mass	1322-1419	125-77, 333
Merit	1021-22, 1036, 1038-41, 1051, 1053, 1821, 2010-11, 2016, 2027	95-103
Mortal and venial sin	1033, 1849-1876	74-76, 84-86
Obligatory attendance at Mass	1389, 1412, 2042, 2181, 2192	130-31

Subject Index

Notes

1. *New York Times,* February 1, 1990, B4.

2. Pope John Paul II, *Salvifici Doloris.* See also *Catechism of the Catholic Church,* nos. 618, 964, 1505, 1521, 1532.

3. Liturgy of the Mass, the Penitential Rite.

4. Quoted by Pope John Paul II, *Crossing the Threshold of Hope* (New York: Knopf, 1995), p. 146.

5. *Catechism of the Catholic Church,* no. 1128.

6. Reported by the Scripps Howard News Service and carried in the *Oakland Tribune,* November 19, 1994, A16, in an article titled "Catholic Priest Dies from Heart Attack in Gay Bathhouse."

7. *The Code of Canon Law,* canon 1247.

8. Thomas Day, *Why Catholics Can't Sing* (New York: Crossroad Publishing Company, 1990), p. 3.

9. Thomas Day, *Why Catholics Can't Sing,* p. 82, quoting Mark Searle, "The Notre Dame Study of Catholic Parish Life," *Worship,* vol. 60, no. 4 (July 1986).

10. Thomas Day, *Why Catholics Can't Sing,* p. 82, quoting Mark Searle.

11. Jessa Vartanian, "A New Leaf," *San Jose Mercury News,* January 19, 1997, G2. Used with permission.

12. *The Rites of the Catholic Church* (New York: Pueblo Publishing Co., 1990), vol. 1, pp. 1077-78.

13. *The Rites of the Catholic Church,* vol. 1, p. 1076.

14. *The Rites of the Catholic Church,* vol. 1, p. 1076.

15. *The Rites of the Catholic Church,* vol. 1, p. 946.

16. Council of Florence, session 11. See also *Catechism of the Catholic Church,* no. 1026.

17. *Christianity Today* (March 6, 1995).

18. *A Catechism for Adults,* Rev. William J. Cogan, Cogan Productions, 1975, p. 50.

19. Second Vatican Council, "Sacred Liturgy," On Holy Communion and the Worship of the Eucharistic Mystery Outside of Mass, no. 79.

20. Second Vatican Council, "Sacred Liturgy," *Instruction on Facilitating Sacramental Eucharistic Communion in Particular Circumstances,* introduction.

21. The Memorial Prayer of the Third Eucharistic Prayer.

22. *Catechism of the Catholic Church,* no. 1374, quoting the Council of Trent.

23. *Catechism of the Catholic Church,* no. 1384.

24. *Catechism of the Catholic Church,* no. 621.

25. Liturgy of the Eucharist, Preparation of the Altar and the Gifts.

26. Liturgy of the Eucharist, Eucharistic Prayer I.

27. *Catechism of the Catholic Church,* no. 1374.

28. John A. McHugh, O.P., and Charles J. Callan, O.P., trans. *The Roman Catechism: The Catechism of the Council of Trent* (Rockford, IL: Tan Books and Publishers, 1982), p. 228.

29. Second Vatican Council, "Sacred Liturgy," *On Holy Communion and the Worship of the Eucharistic Mystery Outside of Mass*, no. 6.

30. *Catechism of the Catholic Church*, no. 1381, quoting Thomas Aquinas.

31. John A. McHugh, O.P., and Charles J. Callan, O.P., trans. *The Roman Catechism: The Catechism of the Council of Trent*, p. 239.

32. "Many Catholics Disagree on Transubstantiation," *Catholic Voice*, June 15, 1992.

33. Quoted by Thaddine Chopp, "Devoted Once More," *Our Sunday Visitor*, November 24, 1996, p. 20.

34. Liturgy of the Eucharist, First Eucharistic Prayer, the Memorial Prayer.

35. *The Memorial Prayer, Eucharistic Prayer III*.

36. Under the Code of Canon Law in effect from 1917 to 1983, every altar was to be constructed with a small space, called the *sepulcher*, into which were to be placed the relics of saints (Code of Canon Law of 1917, canon 1198, section 4). Current Canon Law states: "The ancient tradition of keeping the relics of martyrs and other saints under a fixed altar is to be preserved according to the norms given in the liturgical books" (Code of Canon Law of 1983, canon 1237, section 2). No longer must relics be placed *in* the altar; *under* is sufficient. A movable or portable altar is now exempt from the requirement.

37. *The Memorial Prayer, Eucharist Prayer IV*.

38. Second Vatican Council, "Sacred Liturgy," *Second Instruction on the Proper Implementation of the Constitution on the Sacred Liturgy*, no. 12.

39. Pope John Paul II, p. 139.

40. Pope John Paul II, p. 139.

41. Pope John Paul II, p. 139.

42. Second Vatican Council, "Life of Priests," no. 13. See also the Code of Canon Law, canon 904.

43. Pope John Paul II, *Crossing the Threshold of Hope*, p. vi.

44. Pope John Paul II, *Crossing the Threshold of Hope*, p. 3.

45. Pope John Paul II, *Crossing the Threshold of Hope*, pp. 3-4.

46. Pope John Paul II, *Crossing the Threshold of Hope*, p. 4.

47. Pope John Paul II, *Crossing the Threshold of Hope*, p. 4.

48. Pope John Paul II, *Crossing the Threshold of Hope*, p. 4.

49. Pope John Paul II, *Crossing the Threshold of Hope*, p. 6.

50. Most Roman Catholic titles of religious office are prohibited by Matthew 23:6-10. These include *father, abbot* (meaning "father"); *doctor* (meaning "teacher"); *monsignor* (meaning "my lord"); and *pope* (meaning "father"). This can create some awkward situations for Christians who interact frequently with Catholics and yet wish to obey the Lord's command. Some priests will allow non-Catholics with whom they are well-acquainted to address them by their first names. Another alternative is to substitute *reverend* ("worthy of respect") for *father*. This is an acceptable alternative among Catholics. However, though *reverend* is not explicitly forbidden by the letter of Matthew 23:6-10, it may be by the spirit of the command. In my writings, I have chosen for the sake of clarity to refer to Catholic clergy by their common Catholic titles, seeking to communicate how they think of themselves and how others generally refer to them. In my personal interaction with Catholic clergy, I avoid the use of all religious titles.

51. Second Vatican Council, "Dogmatic Constitution on Divine Revelation," no. 21.

52. Second Vatican Council, "Dogmatic Constitution on Divine Revelation," no. 10, or see *Catechism of the Catholic Church*, no. 95.

53. *Catechism of the Catholic Church*, no. 113.

54. The German Bishop's Conference, *The Church's Confession of Faith* (San Francisco, CA: Ignatius Press, 1987), p. 45, quoting J. A. Möhler. See also the Second Vatican Council, "Dogmatic Constitution on Divine Revelation," no. 8; and the Council of Trent, session 4, "First Decree: Acceptance of the Sacred Books and Apostolic Traditions."

55. Jean Bainvel, *The Catholic Encyclopedia* (New York: Robert Appleton Co., 1912), "Tradition," vol. 15, p. 9.

56. Second Vatican Council, "Dogmatic Constitution on Divine Revelation," no. 9.

57. Second Vatican Council, "Dogmatic Constitution on Divine Revelation," no. 9.

58. *Catechism of the Catholic Church,* no. 108, quoting the Second Vatican Council, "Dogmatic Constitution on Divine Revelation," no. 11.

59. Cardinal Joseph Ratzinger, *Current Doctrinal Relevance of the Catechism of the Catholic Church,* October 9, 2002.

60. Some have accused evangelical Christians of using similar circular reasoning in arguing for the authority and inspiration of Scripture when they say things such as, "I know the Bible is inspired because it says it's inspired." Such reasoning, critics point out, is fallacious. The point is well-taken. Nevertheless, there are valid reasons for believing in the authority and inspiration of the Scriptures. As others have demonstrated, ultimately it is Jesus Christ who establishes the Bible as the inspired and authoritative Word of God. The argument goes as follows: Textual and historical evidence show the New Testament to be a reliable and trustworthy document. In the New Testament is found a record of events related to the life and teachings of Jesus Christ. These provide sufficient evidence to believe with confidence that Jesus Christ is the Son of God. Jesus Christ as the divine Son of God is an infallible authority. He taught that the Scriptures are the Word of God. As the Word of God, the Bible is infallible, supremely authoritative, and utterly trustworthy.

61. *Catechism of the Catholic Church,* no. 119, quoting the Second Vatican Council, "Dogmatic Constitution on Divine Revelation," no. 12.

62. *Catechism of the Catholic Church,* no. 113.

63. The story of Scott Hahn's conversion to Roman Catholicism is based on a book by Scott and Kimberly Hahn, *Rome Sweet Home* (San Francisco: Ignatius Press, 1993), pp. 67-68, 91, and an audiotape by Scott Hahn, *Protestant Minister Becomes Catholic* (West Covina, CA: Saint Joseph Communications).

64. Hahn, *Protestant Minister Becomes Catholic,* audiotape message.

65. Hahn, *Rome Sweet Home,* p. 67.

66. Hahn, *Protestant Minister Becomes Catholic,* audiotape message.

67. Pope Leo XIII, *Adiutricem Populi.*

68. Pope John Paul II, *Crossing the Threshold of Hope,* p. 221.

69. Pope Pius IX, *Ineffabilis Deus.*

70. John A. McHugh, O.P., and Charles J. Callan, O.P., trans. *The Roman Catechism: The Catechism of the Council of Trent,* p. 46.

71. Pope Benedict XV, *Inter Sodalicia.*

72. Pope Pius X, *Ad Diem Illum Laetissimum,* no. 13.

73. *Catechism of the Catholic Church,* no. 2677.

74. Cardinal Joseph Ratzinger, homily, funeral Mass of Pope John Paul II, April 8, 2005.

75. Pope Benedict XVI, address to the College of Cardinals in the Sistine Chapel, April 20, 2005.

76. Hahn, *Rome Sweet Home,* p. 67.

77. Combined quotes from Hahn, *Rome Sweet Home,* pp. 67-68, and Hahn, *Protestant Minister Becomes Catholic,* audiotape.

78. Hahn, *Protestant Minister Becomes Catholic,* audiotape message.

79. Combined quotes from Hahn, *Rome Sweet Home,* pp. 67-68, and Hahn, *Protestant Minister Becomes Catholic,* audiotape.

80. Hahn, *Rome Sweet Home,* pp. 67-68.

81. Hahn, *Rome Sweet Home,* p. 67.

82. *Catechism of the Catholic Church,* no. 893.

83. *Catechism of the Catholic Church,* no. 888.

84. *Catechism of the Catholic Church,* no. 888.

85. Second Vatican Council, "Dogmatic Constitution on Divine Revelation," no. 10.

86. *Catechism of the Catholic Church,* no. 87.

87. Hahn, *Rome Sweet Home,* p. 67.

88. Hahn, *Rome Sweet Home,* p. 67.

89. *Catechism of the Catholic Church,* no. 100.

90. Archbishop John R. Quinn, lecture at Campion Hall, Oxford, June 29, 1996.

91. Pamela Schaeffer, "Initiative seeks 'Catholic Common Ground,'" *National Catholic Reporter,* August 23, 1996, p. 3.

92. "This Fractious Family Wants to Sit Down and Talk," *National Catholic Reporter,* October 13, 1995, p. 20.

93. Cardinal Joseph Bernardin, August 12, 1996, published on the Internet at www.ewtncom/ library/BISH-OPS/COMGROUN.HTM.

94. Quoted by Schaeffer, "Initiative Seeks," p. 3. "Response to 'Called to Be Catholic'" by Cardinal Bernard Law is available on the Internet at www.ewtncom/library/BISHOPS/ COMGROUN.HTM.

95. Quoted by Schaeffer, "Initiative Seeks," p. 3.

96. Quoted by Schaeffer, "Initiative Seeks," p. 3.

97. Andrew M. Greeley, *The Catholic Myth* (New York: Charles Scribner's Sons, 1990), p. 3.

98. Andrew M. Greeley, *The Catholic Myth,* p. 4.

99. Andrew M. Greeley, *The Catholic Myth,* p. 6.

100. George R. Szews, ed., *Why I Am Catholic* (Chicago: ACTA Publications, 1996).

101. George R. Szews, ed., *Why I Am Catholic,* pp. 39-40.

102. George R. Szews, ed., *Why I Am Catholic,* p. 24.

103. George R. Szews, ed., *Why I Am Catholic,* p. 26.

104. George R. Szews, ed., *Why I Am Catholic,* pp. 8-9.

105. George R. Szews, ed., *Why I Am Catholic,* p. 44.

106. George R. Szews, ed., *Why I Am Catholic,* p. 12.

107. Second Vatican Council, *Dogmatic Constitution on the Church,* chapter 2, no. 14.

108. *The Canons and Decrees of the Council of Trent,* Sixth Session, "Decree Concerning Justification," canon 9.

109. Second Vatican Council, "Dogmatic Constitution on the Church," no. 51.

110. Keith A. Fournier, *Evangelical Catholics* (Nashville, TN: Thomas Nelson Publishers, 1990), p. 65.

111. Keith A. Fournier, *Evangelical Catholics,* p. vi.

112. Charles Colson, *The Body* (Dallas: Word Publishing, 1992), p. 265.

113. Charles Colson and Richard John Neuhaus, *Evangelicals and Catholics Together: Toward a Common Mission* (Dallas: Word Publishing, 1995), p. xi.

114. J.I. Packer, "Why I Signed It," *Christianity Today,* December 12, 1994, p. 35.

115. Colson and Neuhaus, *Evangelicals and Catholics Together,* p. ix.

116. Colson and Neuhaus, *Evangelicals and Catholics Together,* p. xiii.

117. J. I. Packer, "Why I Signed It," p. 36.

118. J. I. Packer, "Why I Signed It," p. 36.

119. J. I. Packer, "Why I Signed It," p. 36.

120. *Catechism of the Catholic Church,* no. 882.

121. Second Vatican Council, "Decree on Ecumenism," no. 4.

122. As cited at the World Council of Churches website www.wcc-coe.org/wcc/who/index-e.html.

123. The Augsburg Confession, article 4, "Justification."

124. Council of Trent, session 6, "Decree on Justification," chapter 16.

125. Council of Trent, session 6, "Decree on Justification," chapter 4.

126. Allen, John L., Jr., "Vatican Laments 'Weakness' in German Church," *National Catholic Reporter,* March 30, 2001, p. 4.

127. Allen, John L., Jr., "Vatican Laments 'Weakness' in German Church," *National Catholic Reporter*, March 30, 2001, p. 4.

128. The Code of Canon Law, canon 1364. The Church defines *apostasy* as "the total repudiation of the Christian faith" (canon 751). *Heresy* is "the obstinate post-baptismal denial of some truth which must be believed with divine and catholic faith, or it is likewise an obstinate doubt concerning the same" (canon 751). *Schism* is "the refusal of submission to the Roman Pontiff or of communion with the members of the Church subject to him" (canon 751).

Other Resources for Sharing the Good News with Catholics
by James McCarthy

WHAT EVERY CATHOLIC SHOULD ASK
This 32-page booklet answers 14 questions every Catholic should consider, including, Can you know you're going to heaven? Why did Jesus come? Why did Jesus die? What must I do to be saved? Designed to appeal to the Catholic mind, this booklet provides a positive presentation of the gospel.

THE GOSPEL ACCORDING TO ROME
This insightful examination of Roman Catholicism provides a side-by-side comparison of Scripture with the new *Catechism of the Catholic Church*. Fully documented, this 400-page book focuses on the doctrines of salvation, the Mass, Mary, and authority. Chapter introductions are designed to give readers a feel for what it is like to be a Catholic. A valuable resource for anyone who wants to understand Catholicism and know why the gospel according to Rome is not the gospel of the New Testament.

WHAT YOU NEED TO KNOW ABOUT ROMAN CATHOLICISM—
QUICK REFERENCE GUIDE
This 16-panel guide to Roman Catholicism is a full-color, fold-out summary of *The Gospel According to Rome*. Professionally designed, it includes a list of the 62 major errors of Roman Catholicism, a color diagram and explanation of the Catholic way of salvation, and advice on how to help Catholics. It is ideal for slipping into your Bible so you can be prepared to speak to Catholics at a moment's notice. Consider getting a copy for each family in your church so that they too might be equipped.

LETTERS BETWEEN A CATHOLIC AND AN EVANGELICAL
Roman Catholic priest John Waiss and evangelical minister Jim McCarthy openly discuss their differences in this friendly exchange of letters. Topics include: Is God's Word Scripture alone or Scripture plus Tradition? Who has the authority to teach and rule the church? How is one saved? What is the meaning of the use of bread and wine in Christian worship as instituted by Christ? In this unique book, you'll get both sides of the debate.

CATHOLICISM: CRISIS OF FAITH (RELEASED ON DVD 2005)
This fast-paced 54-minute video documentary examines the teachings of the modern Roman Catholic Church. Includes interviews with several former priests and nuns. Learn how each faced a personal crisis of faith and emerged with a life-changing experience of Jesus Christ. Uplifting and sensitively produced, this film is an ideal educational or evangelistic resource. This is a multilingual documentary with audio tracks in English, Spanish, German, Polish, Korean, Portuguese, Tagalog, and subtitles in Chinese.

HARVEST HOUSE
PUBLISHERS